# unashamed

D1022756

Catherine,

Thank you for being one of the first "readers" of this book! You are a gift from above!

♡ Tracy

# unashamed

CANDID CONVERSATIONS ABOUT
DATING, LOVE, NAKEDNESS *and* FAITH

TRACY LEVINSON *and* FRIENDS

Throughout the book you will find Scripture references that provide deeper insight and support for my thoughts and comments. My hope is that you will look at these verses as led by the Spirit and take time to notice the context surrounding them.

My personal favorite translations:
- The Message - paraphrase
- NLT - New Living Translation
- NASB - New American Standard Bible
- NKJV- New King James
- AMP - Amplified Bible

Copyright 2016 – Tracy Levinson. All rights reserved.

All rights reserved. No part of this publication may be reproduced, stored in a retrieval system, or transmitted in any form or by any means—electronic, mechanical, photocopying, recording, or otherwise—without prior permission from the author.

Scripture quotations marked The Message are from THE MESSAGE. Copyright © by Eugene H. Peterson 1993, 1994, 1995, 1996, 2000, 2001, 2002. Used by permission of Tyndale House Publishers, Inc.

Scripture quotations marked NLT are taken from the Holy Bible, New Living Translation, copyright ©1996, 2004, 2007, 2013 by Tyndale House Foundation. Used by permission of Tyndale House Publishers, Inc., Carol Stream, Illinois 60188. All rights reserved.

Scripture quotations marked NASB taken from the New American Standard Bible®, Copyright © 1960, 1962, 1963, 1968, 1971, 1972, 1973, 1975, 1977, 1995 by The Lockman Foundation Used by permission. www.Lockman.org.

Scripture quotations marked NKJV are taken from the New King James Version®. Copyright © 1982 by Thomas Nelson. Used by permission. All rights reserved.

Scripture quotations marked AMP taken from the Amplified® Bible, Copyright © 1954, 1958, 1962, 1964, 1965, 1987 by The Lockman Foundation Used by permission." (www.Lockman.org)

ISBN: 978-0-692-60598-1

Library of Congress Control Number:  2016900789

PRINTED IN THE UNITED STATES OF AMERICA

Cover Design: Anne-Marie Coffee
Interior Layout: Russell Lake - SeedStudios.com

First Edition

# unashamed

**unashamed**

"*unashamed* is a book that touches hearts and challenges lifestyles. Tracy Levinson tackles relevant issues that go unaddressed all too often. Tracy possesses a genuine transparency that resonates through her personal walk with the Lord. This book is an incredible reminder about how we can be unashamed in Christ's light!"

– JOE WHITE
President of Kanakuk Camps
Author of *Pure Excitement*

"I love this book because it made me feel like I wasn't crazy. I felt like I was welcomed into an open conversation about what felt like were some super dark secrets of mine. I was surprisingly and refreshingly reassured that I am not the only one that desperately seeks companionship, has dabbled in sin, and often questions where I stand with Jesus. Instead of getting a list of religious practices to apply, I felt like I was being transformed as I read unashamed. This book helped me put into words what I had been feeling and what I should be believing. I truly have a better understanding of the Father's heart and hope for my future."

– CARLEE GREEN
College Student, Texas A&M

"*unashamed* is a must-read for all Christian singles seeking love and left pondering the question, 'how?'. This book is invaluable, honest, in-depth and an accurate look into the culture of dating by offering multiple perspectives. Reading—and following—this books' motive will certainly help people in the dating culture, not only to better their dating, but also themselves."

– CHAD HUDSON, young professional

**unashamed**

"This book will make you blush, but you'll be relieved somebody finally had the nerve to say it out loud. Young women are drowning in the waves of culture, desperately seeking answers to the complex questions regarding sexuality. Tracy offers an authentic voice, sharing her own journey out of shame, to a fully redeemed and loved woman of God. She confronts specific questions from real girls and answers them with grace and truth. I will share this book with every young lady I have the privilege of mentoring."

– SHARON MANKIN
Founder of Coffee Talk, a mentoring ministry
and leader to young ladies for more than 25 years

"*unashamed* is so vital in this hour, where young women are facing an onslaught of sexual pressures and expectations like never before. Not only is Tracy open, honest and relevant, she is also daring and willing to expose her own hurts and past in a way that will speak volumes to both young women and young men. I loved how she incorporated the message of God's grace into the theme of the book, and took a valuable opportunity, halfway through - when she has their attention and their trust - to introduce them to the New Covenant in a pure and simple way. As the father of a 10-year old girl, this is exactly the kind of material that I want to put into her hands in the next few years."

– PAUL WHITE
www.paulwhiteministries.com
Author of *Between the Pieces*

"Whether you are a young woman, brother, boyfriend, mom, or dad who loves his daughter, you will love this book. For so many of us, our concept of love and sex comes from culture and tradition, not what the heart of Scripture actually teaches. *unashamed* has a beautiful way of cutting through the religious rhetoric and sheds a light on God's heart. This message is a profound tool to help girls find freedom and release them from being fearful of their own sexuality."

— AMY FORD
President and Co-founder of Embrace Grace
Author of *A Bump in Life*

"This book is long overdue. Today's books on this subject seem to come from two very different perspectives. There is the secular viewpoint where the gritty realities of what sexuality looks like for young adults in the 21st century are honestly and openly explored, but with few solutions or hope. And then there is the faith-based perspective where truth is often dispensed in a way that is not relevant and/or ignores the hard and complex issues that young people actually face today. Tracy brings the best of these together in this wonderful book by offering a real and authentic look into issues and questions that young people have today around their sexuality and providing biblical wisdom into how to navigate this season in a way that is not only practical, but points them towards living out a life that ultimately honors God. I highly recommend this book for those young people who are wanting real answers to real questions and to those who parent them and are looking for ways to discuss these issues in a healthy, open and honest manner."

— CRAIG PIERCE
Owner of The Pierce Academy of Coppell
Preaching team member of Irving Bible Church

# unashamed

"Oh my - this is a powerful book. Honest and raw, it speaks to today's young people. I think every Christian young woman needs this. Her enthusiasm for true transformation in Christ is contagious, and her message is open and honest. Tracy takes the truths of God's word and applies them to the very real and raw issues in our culture today. Fun, uplifting and engaging - the message of *unashamed* reaches into the heart and points to the cross."

— KAROL LADD
www.PositiveLifePrinciples.com
Author of *Positive Life Principles for Women*

"*unashamed* is the conversation every parent wants to have with their daughter, but often finds it too difficult. Frankly and humorously, Tracy Levinson flips over all the rocks that young women would do well to explore to understand themselves, their sexuality, and the choices that will build a better future. Thoughtful, caring, and biblically based, she walks a glorious line to uphold a young woman's purity in God's eyes even as they struggle with temptation and failure. You'll want your daughter to read this book, and perhaps even join her."

— WAYNE JACOBSEN
www.lifestream.org author of *The Naked Church*

"Where in the world was Tracy Levinson when I was in college? I am so thankful *unashamed* will be available for my daughters. What an incredible resource for women of all ages! It's exciting to think where these conversations will lead young women - from questions to confidence in love and dating."

— COURTNEY DEFEO
Creator of Lil Light O' Mine
Author of *In This House, We Will Giggle*

"I couldn't put this book down. I read it in two sittings. Tracy's transparency reminded me of Brennan Manning's, *Abba's Child*. Tracy has taken the issues with which every member of the human race must face, draws us in and empowers us to, through the power of the Holy Spirit, win! Instead of feeling defeated, she inspires; instead of preaching, she transparently ministers. This book took real courage to write, way to go Tracy! I hope *unashamed* goes viral – maybe in several languages."

DR. RODNEY HAIRE
President and Founder
Liberty Christian School, Argyle, Texas
Author of *Called to the Principal's Office*
and *The Diary of Eli*

"In a world inundated with self-help books and personal blog postings, it is truly refreshing to have words shared that answer the questions that are being asked by young women everywhere. I have had the honor of serving students and parents for almost 30 years. The more complicated our culture gets, the greater the need for Truth to be shared. As a father, husband, and minister, I endorse the Truth found throughout this book. Do not read this if you are not prepared to honestly dive into the culture of the day. The battle is real, but our Redeemer is victorious. Our culture will be changed, when our young people walk in this truth. That is what this book is all about. Thank you Tracy, for walking in obedience and boldly sharing from a heart that is saturated with the love of God, and is squeezed out to affect so many."

– JON BROOKS
Student Pastor at Faith Christian School, Grapevine, Texas

"If you are daring enough to finally have those difficult but vital conversations about relationships, sex, faith and intimacy with someone you can trust, choose Tracy and *unashamed*. In a style that reminds me of a challenging, focus-commanding workout that is both breath taking and invigorating, Tracy shares what I want my daughters to know, but I don't have the guts to tell them."

– RALPH HARRIS
Author of *God's Astounding Opinion of You*
President of LifeCourse.org

"Tracy Levinson offers women grace-filled answers to important life questions about dating, love, and sex. Her writing expresses the heart of Jesus Christ like no other work I've seen on this topic. So if you want to infuse solid, Scriptural truth into your romantic life, without the legalism that so often kills the fun, get this book. It's a genuine game-changer!"

– ANDREW FARLEY
Lead Pastor at ChurchWithoutReligion.com,
Bestselling author of *The Naked Gospel*

**unashamed**

This book is dedicated to my family;
Bruce, Josh, and Caroline.
Thank you for loving Jesus.

Thank you for allowing me to be so
authentic about all of our lives and
to tell your stories.

You are so secure in Christ that
you are unashamed because of His grace.

And, to all the girls I've loved,
the girls I will love, and the girl that I was.

**unashamed**

# contents

**unashamed**

# foreword

John Sheasby

Hooray for *unashamed!* Hooray for Tracy Levinson! Hooray
for this book, which will free young people from living in the
darkness and despair that a wrong understanding of God, His
covenants, and His creation of sex have produced in many.
If only this book had been placed in my hands as a young
teenager years ago grappling with these issues in a legalistic
climate of books that told me "thou shalt not…!" about
almost everything pertaining to sexuality.

     What those books did not understand was that the
law was never designed to free anyone from sin's power. In
fact, God designed it to have the opposite effect! Rules
incite rather than curb sin. What gives sin its power is the
law (1 Corinthians 15:56). A book on sex that says: "Don't do
that!" is not going to help anyone get free, but will only serve
to empower destructive behavior and compound feelings of
shame and guilt.

     I love that Tracy has captured the heart of the Father
in His creation of a gift so beautiful and uplifting. You will not
find yourself cringing with shame and guilt as you are told how
rotten you are to have ever even had a bad sexual thought.
Instead, the Father's kindness and comfort will wrap around

your heart as you are carried by Tracy's nourishing words through her own journey from darkness to light. My experience tells me that destructive behavior is rooted in distorted identity. Tracy has given us crystal-clear insight in discovering our new identity in Christ out of which Christ-like behavior emanates. You become a new person through faith in the good news of the Gospel and then through His Spirit living in you, your behavior changes to reflect your new identity. As Tracy has pointed out, trying to change yourself is impossible. God is the one who does the changing by His grace.

Tracy is supremely qualified through her own journey from promiscuity to purity, from law to grace. I have watched Tracy be willing to lay down her ministry to allow the Holy Spirit to reveal and then actualize grace in her life. With that actualization came a rebirth in her marriage to Bruce. My wife Bev and I have thoroughly enjoyed the profound times of honest interaction with them. It has been fun for us to have friends who can talk about sex in an unstuffy, unreligious way. You will be equally blessed by following their journey and exploits in their helpful website www.outsidethenest.net, in addition to reading Tracy's insights in this book. I am excited to have *unashamed* to place in the hands of my granddaughters from someone who I esteem so highly and who "gets it" in the area of sexuality in which so many young people have their darkest struggles.

Through this book, my granddaughters, Ava and Emma, as well as you will embark on an adventure of believing the truth that will free you from shame and guilt and empower you to live *unashamed!*

**unashamed**

# introduction

Another heart-broken, single, young professional was on the other end of my phone, calling me hung-over in tears from waking up naked in a stranger's bed. Or a tear-stained college student ringing my doorbell, wanting to go on a walk to talk about having slipped back into having sex with her abusive boyfriend—the one she finally gained the courage to break up with a month ago.

Then, there was the beautiful woman who sat on my porch, having just gotten married and so unsure about her sex life. The one who grew up in a strict Christian home, tormented about the very existence of her sexuality. This woman, in her attempt to maintain "purity," had trained herself to squelch any attraction or desire for the opposite sex, which sadly now included her new, darling husband. The uneasiness in her eyes, made me think of grown women I know today, women who have never been able to retrain their brains to think their sexuality is anything but "bad." I know ladies who are apathetically uninterested in getting naked with their own husbands.

Texts, phone calls, emails, porch dates, walks, sushi, and girls…lots of girls.

After these encounters my husband would say: "Why are all these young women reaching out to you?"

I would respond, "Probably, because I don't judge them, and because I really care."

All these delightful young women had one thing in common: shame.

I was a new empty nester. My soul was feeling restless. I had been asking God about how different my life would be now with our two kids away at college. I sensed God had a good work for me, but I wasn't sure what it entailed. In the middle of the night during the summer of 2014, words began to form in my mind: "Unfold the New Covenant within the context of a sexual purity talk."

Okay, hold on. I know the minute I use the phrase "New Covenant," some of you have no idea what I am talking about. Or, you are assuming that you do. Either way, it might sound super-religious and theological. I don't want that. Here is a slight clue; remember Jesus saying that he was ushering in a New Covenant at the Last Supper as He lifted His glass of red wine? It's the basic idea that through faith, in Christ's work on the cross, your purity is a secure gift from God (Ephesians 2:8-9). It is not dependent on whether or not a boy puts his hand up your shirt. Please don't assume by my confidence in the grace of God that I'm pro-pain, the kind of pain that sin causes. I am not. Otherwise, I wouldn't be writing this book. However, I'm sure about where purity comes from and who maintains it. He is a person and His name . . . well, you can probably guess His name. He was the most unreligious and cool person ever. For the past six years, I have been deeply dissecting the truth of the Gospel. If you want to know immediately how I explain the New Covenant, you can refer to chapter six. I love that chapter. However, right now, I want to talk to you about sex.

Sexuality is one of my favorite things God has created. I love it and I love talking about it. My hope in writing this book is twofold. First, I hope to help free girls who are fearful of their own sexuality, so they can relax with God and enjoy the process of dating, and perhaps, marriage. Secondly, this book is for girls who feel like they have fallen in the ditch of sexual sin. It is my goal for young women to someday be married, naked and unashamed (Genesis 2:25). I pray this intimate conversation can help comfort and heal some of the pain of unwise sexual choices, while at the same time providing a lighthouse of wisdom for the future. Girls, I am smitten with God's *grace* and *truth*, and I want to share with you how I see God's heart for you when it comes to your love life.

Let's talk about you. I realize every person has a unique story. Most girls are like I am; they long to love and to be loved. Some of you have a deep history with guys, a past that has made you feel like crap, and your mind and heart need to be untangled. I can relate. Others have grown up in a well-intentioned spiritual environment, like my young adult children Josh and Caroline. For the latter group, the fact that I just used the word *crap* in the sentence above might bother your Sunday school teacher. I am deeply acquainted with both worlds. Let's be gracious to each group, as I respond to the following questions that were written by real young women that I know. We may have unique backgrounds but the same God can unravel us all…

I wish someone had come transparently, yet gracefully, alongside me as a mentor, friend, and mother figure to help me sort through honest questions I had about dating, love, sex and faith (Titus 2:3-5). The questions you find outlined in this book are real. They come from single girls and women I know and love. In addition to my thoughts, you will hear from young women, perhaps just like you, as well as single and married men on these topics. Hopefully, some of the questions are the very ones you've been wondering about.

So here you have it. A book with real questions from real young women about dating, love, sex--and how they all intertwine with an invisible God. Are you ready? Let's talk about it . . .

Tracy

# unashamed

# chapter one

.

## let's talk about it

Before we go forward, let's go a little backwards.

    I remember sitting in class embarrassed and frustrated because I was the only kid who couldn't read in the third grade. *nfkdusjfu sljfjie mikanuhl:* That's pretty much what the words looked like to me. Finally, I was diagnosed with dyslexia and a severe learning disability. That's what the world calls it. I just say people are wired differently with unique strengths and weaknesses. Reading simply wasn't a strength for me. Traditional school isn't always the best fit for out-of-the-box people, so thank goodness for *Sesame Street*. That's where I eventually learned to read.

    Along with my learning challenges, I did not grow up with any real understanding of spiritual matters. My family was not into God, at all. As a matter of fact, when I realized there was no Santa, I concluded that there must be no God. At the ripe age of seven, I declared myself an atheist. Yes, a full-blown atheist. That means denying the existence of God. So for me, knowing God was something I put off until my early thirties.

But I can tell you this: From the time I was in fifth grade I was *very* interested in guys and romance. I made a lot of poor choices that brought me a lot of pain. But deep in my heart, underneath my flirtations, teenage crushes and inappropriate relationships, I really was not seeking the attention of one guy after another. All I was really looking for was the *right* guy. More than anything else, I always wanted to be a wife and mom.

I finally got my chance, when I met Bruce Levinson. But I'm getting ahead of myself, so back to the story. We met in 1989--two starry-eyed college graduates who had both moved to Los Angeles, California to attend the American Academy of Dramatic Arts. Bruce was a darling Jewish boy from Rochester, New York. Before he landed in L.A., he was five years removed from graduating with a degree in business, and had an incredible job, including a terrific salary along with a company car. Deciding to throw caution to the wind, he abruptly quit his job to give acting school a try. This decision did not make his prudent Jewish mother very happy.

Enter me; a blue-eyed small town girl, who dreamed of a world beyond Texas. I had just graduated from college at the University of Texas and had made it all the way to acting school in Los Angeles, too. Truth be told; before I left Texas, my college boyfriend had broken-up with me. That heart-breaking event catapulted me halfway across the country and cemented my decision to go to acting school.

Boy meets girl. One night, Bruce and I both reluctantly went to a party that neither of us planned to attend. Bruce was talking to some flirty blonde when my friend introduced me to him. I, on the other hand, was "dating" another guy I had recently met in California. This quotation from F. Scott Fitzgerald pretty much sums up what happened that evening: "They slipped briskly into an intimacy from which they never recovered."[1]

There was a connectedness and ease in the midst of our encounter that very first night. We ended up having one conversation that has led to twenty-four years of marriage, at the time of this writing. The unforced rhythm of our communication continues to be the DNA of our dialogue to this day. We have an authentic, fun, deep, loving relationship.

We certainly have had our ups and downs in the story of our marriage. Some of the downs stemmed from our individual sexual pasts. Trust me, I will share more about this in the following chapters.

Let me tell you a little about how Bruce and I came to a faith in Christ.

Remember, I was not a Christian in the early years of our marriage and neither was my Jewish husband. Bruce and I were living in Chicago with our two-year-old son Josh when our daughter Caroline was born. One day I looked down at her tiny little body as I rocked her in my arms, and sensed something profound was missing. I somehow thought, "I know that I love her, but there must be a *greater* love a mother can have for her child." I threw up a quick prayer saying "God, if you're real, please show me." That began a season of seeking the truth about spiritual matters. At the same time, I had a childhood friend named Dan, who was into the God thing. He faithfully prayed for me behind my back and helped me with some of my questions.

---

1  F. Scott Fitzgerald, *This Side of Paradise*

Feeling restless one cold winter day, I packed up my purple double jogger stroller with two tiny snow-suited children. As we reached the park, I noticed a darling young mom reading a book about prayer while her daughter was going down the slide. After we spoke for a bit, I asked her what she was reading. Turns out, she said she wasn't a Christian, but was going to a Bible Study that some pretty cool Christian women created and led for nonbelievers. She invited me. I eventually went.

At the Bible study, I discovered *God is love* (1 John 4:8). Eventually, this former atheist came to believe that Jesus was the Son of God and that this Christ had died for me and my sins. Good thing, because, my list of sins was quite profound, according to me. When I said "yes" to Jesus, I truly sensed a seismic shift in my soul. I have been forever changed since that moment. It was like the light finally came on into my longing heart.

When I became a Christian, Bruce and I were only four years into our marriage. Bruce was genuinely freaked out over my decision. Soon after that, we moved back to Texas, and during that year my Jewish husband and I started spending time in a creative, Bible church where we met genuinely kind people. Bruce is super relational and the graciousness of these new relationships really touched him. He also started reading the *One Year Bible*, and was blown away by the 300-plus Old Testament prophecies that point to Jesus. A year after I put my hope in Christ, Bruce put his faith in Jesus as his Jewish Messiah. After all, Jesus was Jewish, too.

It was a good thing Bruce and I both came to faith in Christ, but even then, I'm not sure our marriage would have made it. The message of the New Covenant embedded in this book, is really what changed both of us. I promise, you will know what I mean by New Covenant when you read the last chapter.

You've probably heard statistics on divorce rates. Actually, divorce may have already affected your life in some sort of painful way. If that is the case, I really care about any pain that might have caused you. Check out this statistic in a 2012 *Huffington Post* article on marital sex: 15% to 20% of couples are in a sexless relationship.[2] That's crazy, right?

I find young women are often intrigued with a seemingly healthy, lasting marriage. More than one girl has asked me, "Do you really still have a good sex life with your husband after all these years?" Although in the early years we struggled, my answer now is, "Yes!" My marriage with Bruce is full of fun, conversation, romance, intimacy, love, and nakedness. Bruce and I love each other deeply. In terms of love and marriage with one man, I'm currently extremely content and happily married, even though we did have a little tiff yesterday (and of course, I was right and he was wrong).

Now, let me share with you a little about our young adult kids, Josh and Caroline. They are both pretty laid back. Except about Christmas: They are obsessed with Christmas. Most of the time Josh has a guitar in his hand, with Caroline nearby singing in one of their mini jam sessions. Caroline and Josh are pretty tight. Their companionship continues as they attend the same college, and while I know life has its seasons, and circumstances shift, I believe and hope they will always be close.

---

2 Cathy Meyer, *Sexless Marriage: When Sex Ends at 'I Do*, Huffingtonpost.com.

You can learn more about our family and our story at www.outsidethenest.net.

In this empty-nester season, Bruce and I are often delightfully surrounded by young adults. I get to hang out regularly with several young women who text me, meet with me for conversation on our porch, exercise with me, or sit across the table from me at a coffee shop. Why do I appreciate these girls? Maybe it's because of their raw authenticity and willingness to look at life through new lenses. Although I don't present myself as a "guru," I'm willing to explore subjects and walk alongside them as we co-wrestle with topics like life-goals, dating, sexuality, and decisions that have caused these young women some level of pain or confusion. Maybe they open up to me because I have my own story to share and perhaps that makes them feel safe.

As you continue through the pages of this book, you will get no condemnation from me. I could most likely beat you in a competition on unhealthy decisions concerning guys and sexuality. Seriously, let's just go ahead and declare me the winner. When I talk with young women who have questions and struggles in these areas, I share as much as I can so they will know I have been there. Since God forgives and remembers our poor decisions no more (Hebrews 8:12), I will spare the gory details. But I hope I'm gaining your confidence, and I hope you can see that in many ways I have been where you are now. I can't offer you all the answers, but through this book I can be a companion and hopefully a voice of wisdom on your journey, helping you avoid some of the painful mistakes I made and encouraging you to lean into a loving God who cares about your future.

# unashamed

# chapter two

# sex and sexuality

I love chocolate. I have been known to eat it before my meals. Since I'm not really into rules, let's start with the questions about sex.

It's a great place to begin...

## Q Am I a bad person for wanting to be physical with someone?

A Psalm 139:14 says that you are "fearfully and wonderfully made" (NKJV). Your body and sexual desires are a gift from God. I recently told my 20-year daughter Caroline that a strong sex drive is a gift you bring into your marriage. It is a good thing. So the question really is: How do I manage my sex drive?

I remember when Caroline was four years old and having temper tantrums. I wish you could have seen it. She was impressive. This little one would fling her tiny body on the

floor, bringing to mind the verb *writhe*. *Writhing* is defined as
"continual twisting, squirming movements or contortions of
the body."[3] Yep, that's what she was doing, and to add to the
drama, she made the most bizarre tribal sounds. Sometimes,
I had to bite my lip to keep from laughing. Although I had
a deep respect for her commitment and passion to these
episodes, I was concerned. We used to listen to a Christian
song that listed the fruit of the Spirit (Galatians 5:22-23). The
last fruit of the Spirit in the song was self-control. When
Caroline was having a spectacular tantrum episode, I would
lean into her tiny ear and say, "Caroline, you need to use your
self-control." She would gasp for breath and in her squeaky
voice cry, "I caaaan't!"

I tend to be a futuristic person with a vivid imagination.
As she was revolting madly on the floor, I would flash forward
to a future drama of our Caroline at sixteen. The scene? She
is in the back seat of a boy's car making-out with him. My
imagination didn't paint a pretty picture; I saw her having a
dilemma. She had to make a difficult choice between two
or more alternatives, each desirable in their own way, while
experiencing normal sexual feelings. I also sensed her lack of
peace about hooking-up with this imaginary dude. Here was
the worst part about it; I imagined her believing the lie: "I can't
help it." Remember, that is what she said to me when I asked
her to stop having a tantrum. Based on the belief that she
could not control herself, she was set up to make a really poor
decision. Scene over.

I am a stubborn girl. Some people call that "resolve."
As I watched my baby girl fling herself on the floor at the age

---

3 The Oxford Pocket Dictionary of Current English.

of four, I made a decision. If it took me twelve long years, until Caroline turned 16, I was determined to teach her that as a Christian, she possesses all the self-control she will ever need. Enough power all day, every day, to say "yes" or "no" to anything. This is true for all believers. Christ's Spirit lives in His children at all times (Colossians 1:27; Galatians 2:20). He is never lacking, and because Caroline is in Christ, Caroline is never lacking (2 Peter 1:3). God promises to never leave her and she is never deficient of self-control. Neither are you-- if you have placed your faith in Christ. Any message to the contrary is a lie.

## Q How far can I go (sexually) before I'm not "pure"?

## A If you are a Christian, you can go as far as you want and remain pure. The impact of sin on your life is another thing. However, you can't exhaust the grace of God (Romans 5:20-21). Your purity isn't gained by your behavior (Romans 3:22). Believers are pure by Christ's work and His work alone. I stand firm in telling you God's grace is like a powerful tsunami and has made believers deeply and permanently pure. However, sin leads to sorrow. And its consequences stink. As a Christian, you have completely and mysteriously died to the power of sin (Romans 6). When we don't live according to what is true about us, the outcome is often painful, and at times devastating.

Is it wise for you to experience sexual behavior outside of a marriage covenant with your husband? No, it's not. I'm living proof of that. I'm serious. Any kind of sexual behavior outside of marriage only leads to sorrow. Even though Jesus paid for all sin, the Holy Spirit who dwells in you, actually grieves when you don't follow God's best, loving counsel for your life (Ephesians 4:30; 1 Corinthians 6:19-20).

Now, back to this whole "purity" talk. I remember being at a party with Christian women a few years back. One mom described how she shared with a young woman who was dating her son that she was counting on her to keep herself and her son "pure." I'm sure the mom meant well and wanted to protect both of them from harm. Although I remained silent, her words made me want to eat chocolate and run around the city pulling my hair out. That message could have potentially communicated to this young woman that her "purity" came from her sexual choices, and that simply is not true. Let's say the mom who delivered that message to that young woman was overweight. I could send her a similar message by implying to her that if she eats too many donuts one day, then she isn't pure either (Philippians 3:19; Proverbs 23:20-21).

Jesus came to give us purity as a gift. Purity is not dependent on our behavior. It is based on His work, not ours. Let me repeat. Christ Himself is our "purity." Purity is secure. Our behavior is no match for the blood of Christ, which was shed and applies to all who believe (Ephesians 2:8-9).

Let's make this personal. His blood has made *you* clean (Hebrews 9:11-28). That's the Gospel, and if you don't get anything else out of this book, please get this. And yes, if you belong to Christ, you receive His Spirit, which gives you the power to make wise choices that will lead you to love, joy, peace, self-control, and ultimately, life (Colossians 1:27; Galatians 5:22-23). God never wants you to hurt yourself.

Therefore, His Spirit would never lead you to sin (Romans 6). Whether you sin or whether you don't, in Christ, your purity is a settled deal (the Book of Hebrews).

Sometimes I struggle with the concept of purity rings. I'm sure there are some cool reasons girls might wear them. I truly don't want to offend anyone who treasures their ring, but I wonder why refraining from sexual activity exclusively is called "purity" in our church circles? I don't wear a "no over-eating" ring, or a "no gossip" ring, or a "no bank-robbing" ring. Why isn't my purity tied to those behaviors? Are you following me here? I think we send young people a watered-down gospel message by tying a ring that symbolizes a "no touching rule," to "purity." Purity is a constant for all believers under all circumstances, and yes, in light of any sin (2 Corinthians 5:21; Romans 3:22).

Imagine a girl at sixteen, who makes one stupid choice with a boy, and she now feels like a fake or a fraud wearing that ring. It's awesome, if she wears one to remind her of the permanent righteousness she received in Christ. But for many girls who have made one unwise choice, the rings just bring shame, because we have given a special purity status to the work of "no touching" (Galatians 5).

Here is the ring I'm so thankful for: His name is the Holy Spirit. He is a ring - an authentic engraved seal that draws a circle around each child of God as His possession (Ephesians 1:13-14). He claims righteousness (or you could say "purity") for each of His children forever.

Q Should I have physical boundaries before marriage besides no sex?

A Before I answer your question directly, let me share a quote that I believe is true: "The chief cause of failure and unhappiness is trading what you want most for what you want right now" (Zig Ziglar).[4]

Yes, deciding ahead of time what you will and will not do before marriage is a good idea. I'm talking about setting boundaries as God leads for yourself before you even enter into a relationship. Once you are in a relationship, you and your boyfriends' sexual appetites are *not* the determining factor for your choices. Also remember, he is not your husband or leader in this area. You are.

What matters most about boundaries is *where* they come from. This is a subtle point, but it really matters. Are your boundaries a list of rules, rules motivated by fear (for example, fear of making God mad)? Or, are they healthy physical guidelines *motivated by love* to keep you from harm's way? When you set boundaries based on the truth that you are completely loved by God and you want to honor that love above any infatuation you might have with a guy, that makes a big difference. And it makes the boundaries easier to keep.

I have friends who did everything they could do sexually except intercourse before marriage so they could "technically" still be virgins on their wedding nights. That is so messed up. This type of thinking reveals a view of God as a cosmic referee. It's as if God is going to give them points for a technical score.

---

4 Zig Ziglar, Zig Ziglar quote, Ziglar.com.

When we think about sex outside of marriage, it is important to ask *why* God wants us to refrain from it. Could it be because of His great love? Rules often stem from fear—fear of God's judgment, fear of people's opinions, and fear of being "impure." I believe this last fear reveals an inferior view of the true Gospel of God's righteousness received by faith. If you follow rules, you can experience pride when you keep them or disappointment when you break them. My hope is that we can establish boundaries by the power of the Spirit that dwells in *all* believers. Let's make choices based on God's wisdom and love. Here is how I see it…

## Fear + Rules = Pride or Failure

## However, by God's Spirit,

## Love + Boundaries = Protection and Peace

**Q** Does the Bible really teach that Christians should wait to have sex before marriage?

**A** Yes, because God is a loving father and wants what is best for us. The Bible really does instruct us to refrain from sex until "the two become one" in a marriage covenant. There's no way to get around that one!

Check out what 1 Corinthians 6:16-20 (The Message) says about this:

*There's more to sex than mere skin on skin. Sex is as much spiritual mystery as physical fact. As written in Scripture, "The two become one." Since we want to become spiritually one with the Master, we must not pursue the kind of sex that avoids commitment and intimacy, leaving us more lonely than ever—the kind of sex that can never "become one." There is a sense in which sexual sins are different from all others. In sexual sin we violate the sacredness of our own bodies, these bodies that were made for God-given and God-modeled love, for "becoming one" with another. Or didn't you realize that your body is a sacred place, the place of the Holy Spirit? Don't you see that you can't live however you please, squandering what God paid such a high price for? The physical part of you is not some piece of property belonging to the spiritual part of you. God owns the whole works…*

Did you read that verse? It is so powerful. Ironically, I have seen Christians try and excuse sex outside of the marriage covenant, by asking, "Did God really say that?" Reminds me of a chick named Eve who was tempted by thinking, *Did God really say not to eat from that tree* (Genesis 3:1)? If you remember the story, that thought got her into all kinds of trouble.

Don't take my word for it. If you are like me and like to go deeper, you can ponder these passages on sexuality listed below. Just keep in mind that the contexts surrounding the verses matter.

*1 Corinthians 6:13-20*

*1 Corinthians 7:1-5*

*1 Corinthians 10:8*

*2 Corinthians 12: 21*

*John 8:1-11*

*Hebrews 13:4*

*Mark 10:6-9*

*Romans 6:12*

*Ephesians 5:3*

*Colossians 3:5*

**Q** **How far is too far?**

**A** I get asked this one a lot. I usually pause…and ask more than once, "Are you really sure you want me to answer that?"

Each time I hear, "Yeah, I do."

So, hesitantly I say something like; Okay, here is the deal…You're not going to like this, and you know I am not a prude. I have a biblical point of view and personal experience that points to the wisdom of what I'm going to say to you. Here we go; Sex is for marriage exclusively and all sexual behavior, including some kinds of heavy kissing, is just preparation for sex. And I am warning you: Preparation for sex is not for you as a single girl.

Do you want me to be more specific? Remember, I am speaking from the standpoint of wanting to protect you, not from wanting you to obey a list of rules. Here it goes... I don't want any guy touching or kissing my daughter's boobs, her vagina, her butt, or kissing her body in any way, unless he is her husband.

You're asking my advice, remember. As for girls, keep your hands off of a boy's thighs and private parts.

Are you wondering about oral sex before marriage? Really? That is not for you. Giving a guy an orgasm? Really? No—and double no. Is that specific enough? His sexual issues are not your responsibility. None of that is for you.

If I sound harsh by being so graphic and real, remember, I'm only sharing my heart for you. I wish someone had cared enough about me to get into my business in this way.

You might be wondering, "Why be so limiting about sexuality, Tracy?" Here is why: All that touching arouses both you and the guy you're with. And it gets your body prepared for sex and wanting to have sex. I have been there. You can't trust yourself once you're aroused. Let's face it, if you don't plan on having sex, I strongly recommend that you avoid getting aroused (Song of Solomon 8:4).

Here is some insight I received in an e-mail from Pastor Bret Martin, a darling young man who got married a few years ago: "Physical contact is an escalator. It's designed by God to go one place...sex."

Flashback to my high school boyfriend, I was young and didn't really have a strong sex drive. I actually said yes to sex, drum-roll please, *because I was weary from months of saying no.* Not my dream scenario. Clearly I didn't think highly of myself at the time. I felt betrayed. Sadly, the person I felt most betrayed by was me.

A significant excuse, which Christian girls use regularly while dating is to green-light sexual activity by telling themselves, "This is the guy I'm probably going to marry." However, the truth is that you are not married and it is unwise for you to be sexual outside of a covenant. It is also unloving for you to tempt a guy in this area.

As for the guy, I get angry when I think about a persistent guy in your life potentially trying to take what is not his by covenant. I guess I should clarify what I mean by covenant. It's a binding agreement or promise between two or more parties. Marriage is a covenant. Your body belongs to you and to your future husband. Exchanging body fluids is a big deal. You wouldn't use another person's toothbrush lightly would you?

I call a physically aggressive guy a "thief" because he steals what does not belong to him. I know the enemy is behind these intentions and temptations (Ephesians 6:12). I want to kick-his-you-know-what for trying to lure you into sexual behavior. I'm a little worked up over this one because I am furious at the thought of someone tempting you and trying to take you. Jesus got really angry in the temple one day… so mad He threw down tables (John 2:13-16). Believers are the temple of God because of the New Covenant (1 Corinthians 6:19-20). God does not dwell in buildings anymore. He dwells in His kids (Acts 7:48; Acts 17:24). So, I want to knock thieves over and have my own fit as well. If a guy pressures you for sexual activity, I know it is your responsibility to use the self-control that God gave you. I do know that. But I also know love protects. Love does not take advantage of people to manipulate others to behave in ways that are relationally unhealthy. If a guy is aggressive toward you, what kind of "love" is he demonstrating? As I type this, I'm almost shaking with the verse "love protects," because it is my heart for you to be protected (1 Corinthians 13:7).

So, back to the no-touching list that I just made on the fly. Notice, this is not a list of rules. I am saying that sexual behavior belongs between a man and a woman in the context of a covenant. When we do things in God's wisdom, it brings life and peace. Girls, sex makes babies. Sex makes a woman vulnerable. Sex can give you painful and deadly diseases. Violent sex can scar your body and rip your tender insides permanently. The enemy of your soul will try to creep memories into your marriage bed. So why would a loving God encourage you to refrain from something that, at times, can feel so good? Because He loves you. Here is what one of my young girlfriends who graduated from college had to say about it in an e-mail she sent to me: "From my personal experience, sex and anything beyond kissing have been the most heartbreaking and painful experiences in my life. I have never felt more out of control and low about who I am. I'm not sure I can even put into words the ways it has torn my heart apart."

This young friend learned the difficult way, like me. I love this young woman and I love you. Please hear my counsel; all sexual behavior belongs exclusively in marriage. Sorry if you don't like my answer, girls, but you asked.

**Q** What do I do if I've already crossed physical boundaries?

**A** I was living in L.A. in my twenties and I had a "kinda-sorta" boyfriend. He is actually the guy I was dating when I met Bruce. Well, you know, my pseudo-boyfriend didn't really want to be exclusive, so there was no real commitment. Wow. I must have had an amazing self-esteem to put up with that kind of crap. Now, it makes me shake my head, because, you know, I was sleeping with him. I'm not going to lie; the physical part was quite exciting and fun. However, I can still see myself lying there, moments after we were together sexually, like in a movie. Each time, and I mean, each time, I would lie there deeply quiet. There was this little tug in my conscience. Then, spontaneously, tears poured down my cheeks. I remember feeling so vulnerable, exposed and deeply unsafe emotionally. The physical nakedness in the relationship didn't balance out the emotional and spiritual nakedness I longed for. I didn't even want to tell you that story, but I know I'm not the first girl who ever felt that way and I won't be the last. Maybe you have even felt that way too. I understand.

Bruce and I never pretended to our kids that we didn't have a plethora of sinful events in our pasts. However, I have never really wanted my son and daughter to read the details of memories that God has forgiven and forgotten. But, I do want you to know that I am not some religious mom spouting off Bible verses. I know the pain of being sexual before it's time. God and I want so much more for you.

Bruce and I were together having great sex recently. In the midst of our intense embrace, his eyes met mine and we paused. Soul to soul, we were extremely present and receiving, accepting and loving each other. Our physical, emotional, and spiritual nakedness collided. This is possible within the safety of our marriage covenant. And guess what? Just as it happened in L.A. all those years ago, tears spontaneously poured down my cheeks. However, this time they were beautiful tears of love stemming from a healthy, healing vulnerability and connection shared with my husband. Redemption.

If you can relate to this question: "What do I do if I've already crossed physical boundaries?" Then I have some questions to ask you in response:

- **What was the reason you decided to experiment sexually?**
- **Was it a physical longing?**
- **Were you curious?**
- **Were you looking for comfort or love?**
- **Were you drinking or high?**
- **Were you bored?**
- **Were you tired of saying no?**

One of my favorite girls says her weakness is the feeling of loneliness. It's good to be aware of the specific circumstances and feelings that increase your vulnerability. She gave me permission to share part of an e-mail saying: "I know what it is like to be so captivated by the idea of love that you lose your way -- to be so emotionally connected to a boy and then be used by him. I have lost friends, family members, and nights of sleep over a relationship that meant very little to the guy I felt was my "soul mate." It's one of my darkest secrets and biggest regrets in my life."

There is so much more involved in sex than a physical act, especially for girls. Sex deeply involves our emotions and minds. Our souls are fragile. One young woman e-mailed me with this observation: "As girls, our souls and vaginas are totally connected. We can't be physical without being emotional, and sometimes our emotions want us to become physical."

Here is what I have to say about that. Don't feel ashamed. But, guess what? Your emotions are not in charge, nor are your physical desires. My friend Amy's four-year old daughter woke up one morning and wanted candy for breakfast. After all, the previous night had been Halloween. Amy said…(drum roll please)…"No!" Because she is the mom and she is in charge. Likewise, you are the parent of your body and emotions. Take care of them and make good decisions for them. "No" can be your very best friend as you protect yourself with love.

Now, I didn't really finish answering this question, did I? Let's do that by answering the next one. The time has come to talk about God's grace (Hebrews 13:9).

**Q** **I have already been involved sexually, so how do I have a redo?**

**A** As I read this question, I am thankful that our daughter will let me tell another story about her. Here's the first part of it.

As a little girl, I was tucking her into bed one night, after she had acted like a total butt that day. I was trying to describe to her how God forgives, so I ran and got a dry erase board and wrote on the board in red what she had done that day. Then I took an eraser and said, "Here is what God did to that sin", and I erased those words until they were invisible. Throughout her childhood, if she asked for forgiveness for something, I periodically took my right hand and erased whatever it was in the air.

Scroll forward, my girl is in high school and had her first boyfriend. They had been dating for several months. Caroline has a very hip bohemian bedroom and she was lying in her cozy bed one school night, while I was hanging out in her room. I can still see her there with her covers pulled up, as she began to tentatively share with me all that had been going on between her and this boy. I call it "the confession night." Bruce was conveniently out of town.

You will hear more about this significant evening in the chapter on boys, because, for some strange reason our son Joshua, unbeknownst to his sister, decided to reveal to me his own struggle that very same night…

Anyway, as the night continued and the confessions poured out, a pause would appear in our conversation. I would start to leave her room. Each time, right before I would crossed the threshold, I would say, "Baby, is there anything else?"

She would say "No."

As I began to pass through the door, she would be brave and say "Well there's one more thing."

And, as Caroline began to share, it was like a tiny stream of dams that were progressively opening up into a flowing river. Some of you girls who are like me and have been around the block sexually, would think her dabble with darkness was small. But to her, it was a really big deal. Remember:

## Lies + Beliefs + Actions = Shame and Pain

I listened and loved her, gave her counsel, and prayed with her. Want to know some of the thoughts I shared with her that night?

"Child, God was with you loving you in the midst of your sin. Darkness is not dark for God" (Psalm 139:12). God loves you so much that your sin grieves the Spirit (Ephesians 4:30) You are completely clean and forgiven. I'm not saying that there are no consequences for sin. God allows discipline for His sons and daughters, and so do I, as a mom. However, He is not mad at you. And for goodness sake, don't believe when the enemy tries to tell you that since you have participated in the sensual that you are in any way tainted, or that your mistake has become part of your identity (Romans 3:22; 2 Corinthians 5:21). Some people are afraid to believe in total forgiveness. But it's the gospel truth. Because of Christ, your sins are paid for and erased" (Hebrews 7:27; Colossians 2:13-14). First John 2:12 says: "I am writing to you who are God's children because your sins have been forgiven through Jesus." (NLT)

Caroline was brave that night. Although terrified, she knew deep down, that keeping things in the dark was not wise. She found a "safe place" to bring dark to light (James 5:16; Ephesians 5:13-16).

I know a darling young girl who got pregnant the summer before her senior year in high school. What do you say to her mom, a dear friend, who is about to watch her baby have a baby? Here is what I said; "Tell her that God still sees her white as snow" (Isaiah 1:18). Hebrews 10:17 says, "I will never again remember their sins and lawless deeds" (NLT).

When our kids were little I had a specific way that I disciplined them. Before they received a spanking, I would say, "Mommy and Daddy spank you because..." and they would respond as taught, "Because you love me." Once again, let me try and keep from being misunderstood. I am not pro-sin. I'm not encouraging sin. I believe there are often terrible consequences for poor choices, and most of the time they stink. Discipline is not fun for any parent or child, no matter how young or how old. But remember, discipline and punishment are two different things. They have different goals. Discipline's goal is to protect and teach. Punishment's goal is to cast judgment or condemnation. Punishment is given through mental, emotional, or physical pain. Jesus was punished on the cross for all your sins (read more about this in chapter six). As a Christian, you're a daughter of God and He disciplines those He loves (Proverbs 3:12, Hebrews 12:6).

So what do I say to a precious girl who has been sexual with boys in the past? It's time to forgive yourself. You do that by agreeing with God that you are forgiven and that He is close.

Know this: God cares deeply about your pain. Pain is pain, even if it was your choice. You perhaps need healing and comfort. My counsel? Find a safe person to confess to (James 5:16); choose someone you believe to be loving and wise. Scripture teaches over and over again to look for wise counsel from people who bear good fruit. So basically, confessing to a friend who is having sex with her boyfriend might not be the most helpful. Find a grace-filled Christian counselor, or a wise believer who is full of love, joy, peace, patience, kindness, and sexual self-control (Galatians 5:22). That would be a good place to start.

## Q How do I stop having sexual feelings?

**A** Well, you can't stop being sexual. God made you that way. But if you're asking, "How do I stop sinning sexually?" I have some observations to share. Have you ever seen a dog eat its own throw up? It's just so gross. Whatever was in that vomit must have made that dog sick. Why eat it again? But that's what dogs do—and we are acting just like them when we repeat foolish and hurtful behavior (Proverbs 26:11).

We have used fear too long in our churches to try and control behavior--fear of God's anger, fear of God's disappointment, fear of God's not being close. As a Christian, God is dwelling in you. Pause on that thought. Take a second to soak that in. We have this weird idea that God takes a vacation when we sin. No! God is always dwelling in us. He loves you at *all* times. His very close presence provides everything you need to overcome temptation (Galatians 5:16). Second Peter 1:3 says: "by his divine power, God has given us everything we need for living a godly life" (NLT).

Let's stop justifying and making excuses for sin. We have died to sin. It is not who we are, and it has *no* power over us. All God's anger toward sin was poured out on the cross (1 Peter 2:24; Romans 5:9). The problem occurs when we don't *believe* this is true. What you believe deeply affects your behavior.

Romans 8:2 says: "And because you belong to him, the power of the life-giving Spirit has freed you from the power of sin that leads to death" (NLT). God is so kind. He says you are clean and righteous. So believe it. If you have to repeat it to yourself a hundred times a day in order to get it ingrained in your thinking, believe it. His pleasure remains satisfied through His Son's sacrifice, accomplished on your behalf. Now you can walk in this reality of being truly free from the power of sin (Romans 3:22). Honestly, in the end, it's actually more fun.

I Corinthians 15:34 says: "Awake to righteousness, and do not sin" (NKJV).

## BELIEVE
God loves you.
God is close.
God wants to protect you.
You are clean.
Sexual expression is for marriage.
Believers have all the power we need over sin.

How do you stop sinning? You stop by stopping. (Hebrews 12:1, Romans 6:11). Here are some practical steps to help believers turn away from sexual sin.
- Forgive yourself.
- Share your story with a safe person.
- Break up with the guy.
- Date guys whose actions demonstrate that they want to protect you sexually.
- Avoid being drunk or high.
- Avoid sensual music and movies. I have a young friend who has a weakness for romantic movies.

*The Notebook* did her in. As dramatic as this may sound, it was like a gateway drug. It stimulated in her a desire for experimentation with boys.

- If being alone is too tempting, be in public with your date.
- If you are involved a healthy, Spirit-led relationship, consider getting married.

I Corinthians 6:18 says: "Run from sexual sin! No other sin so clearly affects the body as this one does. For sexual immorality is a sin against your own body" (NLT).

God is compassionate toward you and patient. My dear friend Colleen wisely says, "Change is difficult. Even with the resurrection life of God working in us – like a Latin dance two steps forward and one step back. I want girls to focus more on the quality of their walk with God than the steps to spirituality. He'll take them through. He is faithful. He began it, and they can bank on Him finishing it."

**Q** **What do you think about modesty?**

**A** This is a funny question for me because I love nakedness. When our kids were babies, Bruce and I used to laugh when they would run around the house naked as jaybirds before bath time. I also adored it when they shook their cute baby bottoms to the tune of "shake your booty!"

Actually, I have been thinking about this subject a lot lately. Pondering the differences between clearly beautiful paintings and sculptures of the naked human body contrasted with the pornography of our day. Why is one so beautiful to me while the other is so destructive and sad? Perhaps, the perversion lies in the intent.

In some parts of Europe, for example, breasts don't create quite the stir that they do here in the U.S. Do they consider breasts the way we do elbows?

I'm just not sure about it all. When Caroline was little I used to take her shopping. At times, I would try on something clearly sexy. And she would always say "Mommy, that's really pretty!" I always wanted my kids to think sex in marriage is fun and something to look forward to. I would respond to her with a big grin and say, "I know. I'm only going to wear it for daddy!" I like to dress however I want. I like to look good for Bruce on a date and push the sexy envelope a bit for special occasions. But, I have never been the kind of wife who wanted men, besides Bruce, to look at me sexually. Back when our marriage was rocky, I remember being very uncomfortable when he would stare at a woman, especially if she was dressed provocatively. I was hurt by his interest, and angry with her disregard for others. I used to joke with girlfriends that I wanted to get a water gun at freezing temperatures and start squirting women who dressed with their boobs hanging out.

One of my dearest friends, Linda, a mom of three has this to say about modesty in an e-mail she sent me:

> "I do not want girls feeling like they need to wear long denim skirts and long sleeved shirts. But, I also feel you do not want to throw your boobs in someone's face. For me, I would ask the Holy Spirit, "Is that appropriate for me to wear?" It is just as easy for a man to lust after a girl in a business suit as a bathing suit. Why is

*someone dressing that way? Usually, it comes from a lack of confidence."*

Sometimes, girls dress immodestly because they think low-cut tops and short shorts are attractive to guys. So, I asked some guys about it. You'll find a male perspective on modesty in chapter three: *what do guys think?*

**Q** **What do you think if I have taken the morning-after pill or had an abortion?**

**A** I had a friend in college who had many abortions. She kept repeating the same patterns over and over. Are you asking what I believe about it? You were bought with a price and your body is meant for life, not death. The Spirit within us grieves when we choose death. If you are in Christ, God's inexhaustible grace was and is provided for you (Romans 5:20-21). You are deeply loved, and He forgave you before it ever happened. God has no desire for you to feel shame or condemnation. But godly sorrow is appropriate. You are still clean and close to God. He doesn't see you as the girl who had the abortion. That act is not your identity. I suggest you find a really good, grace-filled Christian counselor to walk you through the process of forgiving yourself and changing patterns that led you to be vulnerable to pregnancy.

To go deeper into this topic visit:
www.focusonthefamily.com/lifechallenges/love-and-sex/
abortion/abortion and www.embracegrace.com

Q What if my single parent is having unmarried sex?

A I really do know girls who are dealing with this. If this
is you, I am so sorry that you do not have a healthy
example to follow. You're not crazy if it bugs you. Don't justify
it in your mind or somehow think it is cool, because they are
older. If your parent is a safe person, feel free to share your
feelings (Ephesians 4:25). And then let go. Don't become
bitter about it. It's your parent's unwise choice. Forgive them.
Remember, you are your own person and it has nothing to
do with you. You and Christ have your own relationship. Keep
in step with Christ and live your life with Spirit-led decisions
(Galatians 5:25).

Q Can we just talk about masturbation?

A Sure we can. Nobody really talks about it for girls,
especially Christian girls. Our bodies are interesting, are
they not? Now girls, you know I'm not a licensed counselor,
a nurse, or a doctor. So, this is just my opinion. It seems the
Bible is pretty silent on the topic of masturbation. I'm not even
going to label it a sin. So, I don't really want to make a big
deal about it.

I'm super glad if you have a strong sex-drive. What a
gift you can bring into your marriage!

I know there are times you are bored, curious, feeling
sexual, or just needing some comfort. But I don't encourage
the behavior. I believe self-stimulation just wakes up your sex-
drive at a time when it's not helpful and can easily lure you into

sin. Anything that becomes a compulsive pattern in our lives can turn into a big deal. For some, this moves beyond the physical into fantasy or porn where you are playing with lust, which is definitely not for you. Lust is sinful and it will ultimately bring sorrow to your life.

If you have engaged in this behavior, don't be ashamed. As a believer, Christ has made you clean. And in Christ, you have power over this behavior. You have been set free from being a slave (Romans 6). I also think that it can become a habit or secret you bring into your marriage. I don't keep secrets from Bruce. I'm all about intimacy. No secrets. I assure you the love and emotional intimacy that is possible with a husband wins in my book.

If your patterns of behavior are seemingly addictive, stop. I mean it. You can stop. You have all the power you need for that (2 Peter 1:3). As you are moving toward freedom, immediately give yourself grace if you stumble. God has your back. Keep remembering that you are loved and have power in Christ. If you feel you need some help, please find a good counselor to talk with. You've been set free (John 8:36). So find a way to live freely.

**Q** What If sexual abuse is part of my story?

**A** I remember being about nine years old. I had a new friend spend the night at my house. We had a fantastic time. But the next morning, after pancakes and eggs she pulled me aside and began to cry and started begging: "Can I stay longer?"

I asked her, "Why?" And she responded, "If I tell you, would you promise not to tell anyone?"

I childishly said, "Okay." And she began to share how her new teenage step-brother would make her take baths with him. And then she began to describe the behaviors he would make her do. I was little and had never heard of such things, but something in my conscience knew that what she was describing was terribly wrong. I had met the step-brother and I was furious, to the point of shaking. When her mother wouldn't let her stay longer that day, I felt helpless--helpless to protect my friend, helpless because I wanted to tell my mom and I wanted her mom to protect her. But I had bound myself to a promise that I felt trapped to keep. Looking back, I wish I had told my mother.

If you have experienced any kind of abuse, child abuse, incest, or date rape, I want to look you in the eye, put my hand on your arm and let you see the tears rolling down my cheeks. I care deeply. I'm so sorry that happened to you.

I have other friends who struggled with being super-promiscuous early in life. And in each case, someone older had approached them sexually. If this has happened to you, the enemy wants you to walk in shame and steal from you. During the abuse, you might have experienced physical pleasure, and that can be confusing. It is because your body is made to enjoy sexual touch. Do not feel ashamed. Just be determined to tell someone what has happened to you. Tell someone safe and work through your memories, extend forgiveness, and create boundaries for your life. You want to have a healthy marital sex life. You can! But do the work now, so you can start to heal. You'll be glad you did.

To dig deeper into this topic visit:
www.focusonthefamily.com/lifechallenges/abuse-and-
addiction/sexual-abuse/sexual-abuse

........................................................................................................

## Q How do you see the gay issue?

**A** I was a dancer (by the way, not a great one) with an undergraduate and graduate degree in theatre. In my world, I have been blessed to know and meet lots of wonderful people who consider themselves to be "gay." My best friend in graduate school and his partner were mine and Bruce's best couple friends in our early years of marriage. All people are "fearfully and wonderfully made" and my homosexual friends are no exception (Psalm 139:14, NKJV).

Let me clarify something, I am not addressing my comments here to nonbelievers. However, if you consider yourself a Christian, let's chat about this topic.

Maybe you have dabbled in same-sex relationships. Maybe you have experienced gay porn. Maybe you have deep fears about being gay. Or maybe it's not for you, but you believe it is okay for others.

One of my best friends, Leah Springer, who is a Christian counselor, puts it this way: "Your body is wired by God to respond to certain kinds of touch. If you were blindfolded and could not see the gender of a person or their age, your body would respond anyway. You can't look to your body to determine what's for you. Girls often feel bad because their bodies responded to same-sex touch."

I have several amazing, grace-filled friends with whom I'm very close, who respectfully think differently than I do on this subject. I have no desire to offend anyone. Sometimes it seems when you don't encourage homosexuality, you are seen as unloving or too religious. I am none of those things. I'm just an honest girl looking for honest answers.

So the question I'm asking is: From what source are we going to seek truth? Our feelings? Our genitals?

As a former atheist, I often wonder what others think about the Scriptures. There is a difference between having a struggle in this area and claiming that the Bible encourages a homosexual lifestyle. Some out there claim the Bible is cool with homosexual behavior. It's good to question Bible interpretations when your motive is to seek truth. Here are some passages of Scripture that reference homosexuality:

Genesis 19:4-9

Leviticus 18:22; 20:13

Romans 1:24-27

1 Corinthians 6:9-10

1 Timothy 1:9-10

There is a lot of confusion on the topic of homosexuality. Satan is the author of confusion, a deceiver, and a liar (John 8:44). Like the snake said to Eve in the garden, "Did God really say that?" (Genesis 3:1).

The God I am in relationship with is not a God of confusion. I'm not confused about homosexuality at all. I don't know how you can get around it. It's pretty clear in the Bible to me that God considers this behavior 'unnatural', "degrading", and dishonoring. Since God *created* all of nature and *loves* His creation, He should probably know what He is talking about.

Let's look at Romans 1:24-27 together, "Therefore God gave them over in the lusts of their own hearts to [sexual] impurity, so that their bodies would be dishonored among them [abandoning them to the degrading power of sin], because [by choice] they exchanged the truth of God for a lie, and worshiped and served the creature rather than the Creator, who is blessed forever! Amen. For this reason God gave them over to degrading *and* vile passions; for their women exchanged the natural function for that which is unnatural [a function contrary to nature], and in the same way also the men turned away from the natural function of the woman and were consumed with their desire toward one another, men with men committing shameful acts and in return receiving in their own bodies the inevitable *and* appropriate penalty for their wrongdoing" (AMP).

I'm not a girl who can conveniently pick and choose Scriptures to fit what I think they should say. I find questioning the counsel of our loving God in an attempt to justify sin to be a very unwise thing to do. Here is what I think: I definitely believe that same-sex behavior is never God's desire. As a paid-for sin, it falls under forgiveness, just like gluttony and adultery. Because of Christ, God's not freaked out about it. Grace was and is sufficient for the forgiveness of all sin. But if we have died to sin, God says how can we live in it any longer (Romans 5:20-6:1)?

The thing that makes this issue unique is that homosexuality has become more in our culture than just a behavior. It has become a protected identity. I can go a whole year having lots of naked sex with my husband and never think about the fact that I'm a heterosexual. I sometimes overeat, but I don't go to parties and say, "Hi I'm Tracy and I'm a glutton." No way. I am *not* my sin. I am a new creation (2 Corinthians 5:17), a child of God... Beloved. I think that is good news.

I'm in harmony with my pro-gay friends in some important areas. For example, I agree that God loves everyone. I believe people should be treated with dignity. And that it is never okay to be unkind to someone based on their sexuality. But I do have a question. Whose response to homosexuality gives the person involved in this lifestyle more hope? The Christian who says, "I approve. I'm cool with it. I think it's great. Do whatever you feel"? Or, someone like me, whose message includes a vision of freedom from a homosexual lifestyle? If I was struggling with homosexuality, I would be relieved to know that this lifestyle was not my "fate".

I teach theater classes. I'm a simple girl, at times. When my students in drama class bring up the topic of homosexuality or gender confusion, I usually say, "Guys, in the beginning God made the male *and* female (Genesis 1:27)! Do you want to know if you are a boy or a girl? (My middle schoolers are blushing now!) When you get out of the shower look down and you can know for sure.

Let's look at our culture and take this confusion to a whole new level. I remember seeing ABC News report a story of a Canadian family who decided to raise their baby, Storm, with only a few people knowing his or her gender. What was the goal? They decided to let the child decide his/her own sex.[5] And I can't forget the Swedish couple I read about in the *Huffington Post*, who announced they were raising their

---

5  Susan Donaldson James, "*Baby Storm Raised Genderless Is Bad Experiment, Say Experts,*" abcnews.go.com.

kid, Pop, gender-neutral as well. Frida Berrigan, "Who Needs Gender Norms? Not Children -- That's For Sure,"[6] Let's take it a step further: Children as young as nine years old are being given controversial drugs to prepare them for gender transformation surgery.

My husband appreciates the simplicity of God's design. He loves the perfect picture of a man and a woman's sexual organs in marriage fitting together like a puzzle. He marvels at the reality that through that union comes *life.*

What if you have gay thoughts? Here is an excerpt from a text I sent to one of my favorite girls recently, based on John 8:44; "Be aware that the enemy will lie to you and *tell* you what 'you' want. Every idea you have is *not* yours."

Be confident. You have a new heart and a new mind in Christ (Ezekiel 36:26; Jeremiah 24:7; 1 Corinthians 2:16; 2 Corinthians 5:17). All thoughts that lead to ungodly behavior originate from the enemy of your soul, *not* from *you.* If he can get you to think participating in homosexuality is your idea, and you believe him, actions are probable to follow. And next comes shame.

## Lies + Belief + Actions = Shame and Pain

## Satan is the King of Pain.

I have a very dear male friend who is a believer and has wrestled with same-sex temptation for many years. He says:
*Every one of us struggles with some type of 'lust'*
*whether it be with a person (same or opposite sex), or*

---

6 Huffingtonpost.com

*it be a material possession like a throw rug, or a house or a car, or [fill in the blank]. If we are "in Christ" we are a new creation and there is no condemnation to those who are in Christ Jesus! It was all nailed to the cross. Remember, the enemy comes only "to steal, and to kill, and to destroy" (John 10:10, NKJV). We are in this together and we as the body of Christ need to encourage, support, and love one another.*

I don't type these words lightly. If this is your struggle, I have deep compassion for you. Tenderly and confidently I want to say, there is hope and joy for you. Christ has purchased your freedom from homosexual behavior. That's good news! It's not who you are! That's good news! Satan has been messing with you. The ungodly ideas that might float across your mind are from *him*, not from you. He is a liar—the worst of the worst. Be brave, child of God. Get some really good grace-filled Christian counseling and learn to live freely (Romans 6:14). I know this can seem like a daunting task. But remember nothing is impossible with God. And the truth will set you free. You were made by God. Trust Him, not your fears, feelings or memories. Remember your feelings are important to God. But they are not in charge. Take even a mustard-seed size hope that Jesus is serious about His ability to set captives free (Luke 17:6). Believe that step-by-step God can lead you to greater peace and freedom. God made you. He can restore you to walk in His original design. Believe.

To dig deeper into this topic visit:
www.purelifeministries.org and www.pureintimacy.org.

*Lord, would you give wisdom to anyone who reads this chapter on sexuality? I pray they will "test all things and hold fast to that which is good." Unashamed, let them hold fast to every word that is life giving. I pray we will all walk in deeper freedom, in Jesus' name (1 Thessalonians 5:21).*

**_Girls_**,
_I have these periodic moments, as
I'm writing this book.
It is something I have never quite
experienced before.
I find myself thinking of you ...
And remembering the "me" before I
knew Christ.
I find myself struggling to breathe
and spontaneous tears surprise me, as
I envision you reading this.
There is something deep in my
heart: a longing for the girl I used
to be and a desire for you to have
wisdom, protection, peace, and an
assurance of love in Christ.
I guess it is Christ in me. I suppose
it is a piece of God's heart for us girls.
I can barely contain it.
I care deeply about you and your
future...your life...I love you.
I want so much good for you.
His name is **Christ**....
He is real...He is a person...He is
yours....
Do you believe?_

unashamed

# chapter three

# what do guys really think?

I strongly believe that a guy's point of view is imperative in addressing girls' questions about sex and sexuality. But before I let the men have the floor, I want to respond to a specific question, because I really care about the character of the guys you date.

**Q** What should I look for in a guy?

**A** Let me tell a story before I jump into a direct answer. Several years ago our family left the comfort of our small, sweet Texas town and moved to Sunland, California for my husband's job. I don't know what we were thinking...We left the land of "tra-la-la-la-la", big Texas smiles, and wide open spaces, and traded it for sirens, liquor stores, and crystal meth labs disguised as homes. We also encountered young women prostituting themselves on the street and drunken humans laying on the sidewalk as we drove our kids to their new

45

elementary school. I am *not* exaggerating. On the first day at my daughter's new California school, we waited in line outside. There was a darling, shy girl behind her with long blonde hair. I started a conversation with her and she and Caroline became fast friends.

Until about the third month of school, then the tears started. Caroline came home one day and said, "Mom, "what's her face" (I will call her that for the sake of anonymity) has decided that no one should be my friend. So I stand on the playground alone and kids run up to me and say terrible words about me."

"Okay," I said to myself, "Is this a tragedy or an opportunity?" Here is my daughter, ripped out of her sweet Texas cocoon. Now the kids are bullying her? Deep breath, Tracy. First, I listened and comforted her with compassion. I also called the school and asked for some discreet assistance. She won't know I did that until she reads this. Love protects, you know.

What a perfect time that was to encourage my daughter not to place her hope in humans. We spent time together considering that God is a person and that Jesus is actually her best friend (Proverbs 18:21; James 2:23; John 15:15). I wanted to teach her what distinctives to look for in close relationships. In looking toward the future, I thought those same principles we pondered would help her choose her spouse one day. See, I haven't forgotten the question: "What should I look for in a guy?" The same thing I taught her is what I think you should look for in a man.

We decided this was her new criteria for relationships. It's from Galatians 5:22-23 and called the fruit of the Spirit:

- love
- joy
- peace
- patience
- kindness
- goodness
- faithfulness
- gentleness
- self-control

FYI, socially, things began to turn around for her after only a few months.

Knowing the fruit of the Spirit will help you discern the Spirit at work in a guy you might potentially date. There are lots of other ideas to consider in a dating relationship. What does he look like? Is he smart, ambitious, funny, creative, a good conversationalist, athletic, or outgoing? There are a plethora of fun topics to consider. But remember, I encourage you to make sure he has a faith in Christ. If he doesn't, it's a deal breaker.

However, what if at first, that guy acts wonderfully, just as Caroline's friend did in third grade. And then things start to go downhill? Will you be honest with yourself if he starts acting like a jerk? Is this the type of behavior that you're honestly looking for in a guy? Are you willing to give him the boot if his "fruit" stinks? I would advise you that a demonstration of the Fruit of the Spirit is a must. I'm not talking about demanding perfection, but being willing to honestly ask, "What is this guy characterized by?" Ask yourself, is he loving, joyful, peaceful, patient, kind, good, faithful, full of gentleness, and does he exercise self-control, especially in the sexual area? Take your time to discover his character. Don't decide he is the one for you after two dates, or based on his social media posts. Keep testing all things and see if the relationship lines up with God's best for you (1 Thessalonians 5:22). Ultimately, God will give you a peace or lack of it, as He guides you in dating (Colossians 3:15).

Here are some thoughts about men written by a very wise, young, college girl that I love. When I asked her how she would respond to a girl who wants to know what to look for in a guy, she said, "How does he treat the person who serves him his food? How does he treat his parents? When I see a man who respects those around him and treats them with humility and thankfulness, it reflects Christ, living in his heart. Do not flirt to convert, girls. A man will not change his values and personality traits once he is in a committed relationship; if anything, his flaws will manifest themselves in ways that they had previously been hidden."

**Q** What do guys look for in someone they want to date and potentially marry?

**A** I want to introduce you to some fine young men I know. They are normal guys, thus imperfect. But trust me, they are believers in Jesus, darling, fun, kind, full of goodness, loving, insightful, and amazing human beings. They are the kind of guys I would be willing to encourage you to date. You'll see their thoughts intertwined with mine. I will be pondering their responses alongside you.

Mitch: *"I need someone who can see through my junk. I want a woman who isn't afraid of hard times because she is confident in herself and in God. I want to marry an imperfect woman who is forthcoming about her shortcomings, a woman who is not afraid to start difficult conversations or to ask questions she may not want the answer to, a woman I periodically look up from my relationship with and see clearly that she has helped change me into something that more closely resembles our Savior."*

 Chad: *"Confidence, honesty, open with her emotions, has a career, dreams and/or goals, a life outside of the relationship, and the potential to be a best friend. I look for a girl who is beautiful inside and out. She has to be comfortable in various scenarios, whether that means dressing up for a fancy dinner or event, wearing sweatpants and a t-shirt, or sitting on the couch all day."*

Spencer: *Here is my list:*
1. *A super-great friend.*
2. *A good listener.*
3. *Someone who's not set in their ways.*
4. *Joyful.*
5. *Interacts well with others.*
6. *Someone who can move past small talk.*
7. *Loves God.*

Blake: *"I prefer a girl who clearly cares more about her relationship with Jesus than she cares about finding a guy. I don't want to find someone I need to change in order for her to be the person I want to marry. I also am attracted to girls who are spontaneous, optimists, and willing to take risks in order to pursue what we believe the Lord has for us. I'm also looking for a girl who has the character qualities that will make her a great mom."*

Wes: *"Nothing is more attractive to me than a girl who understands that life is a beautiful gift, and wants to use that gift to benefit others. That, plus a sense of wonder and appreciation for the beautiful and terrible world that we live in."*

Barrett: *"I'm looking for someone who has a strong relationship with the Lord and has goals of her own. You also can tell a lot about people by how they treat their own parents/siblings/friends/strangers. I'm attracted to someone who is funny, kind, and a good listener. Somebody I could grow old with remain best friends with until the day we die."*

Chandler: *"Confidence plays a large part in what I look for in a girl. It is not an arrogant sense of superiority, quite the opposite. It comes out as dependence on the Lord. Much of that comes from understanding of the Gospel and what has been done for us. One thing I look for in a girl is that she excels in something she is good at."*

Brandt: "Someone who operates in a high level of love and positivity. A woman who has a God vision, mission, or purpose for her life. Someone who I can trust, have fun with, a best friend."

John: "I look for a girl who doesn't take herself too seriously. A girl who is constantly worrying all the time about everything is a turn off to me, and even shows a lack of trusting God. I also look for gentleness and kindness in a girl. I'm looking for a girl who will encourage me spiritually, love me unconditionally, forgive me relentlessly, and follow my lead as I run to the throne of grace—someone who loves Jesus more than she loves me. Where could more beauty be found than in a girl like that?"

Austin (just married): "The number one thing I looked for in a wife was loyalty. I wanted someone who would stay with me forever, more than I wanted someone who was perfect. I looked for someone who could laugh, someone who could fight, someone who could go on an adventure with me and be okay with it going south. Would she be broken? Maybe. Flawless? Far from it. But she would be mine and no one else's."

What do guys think about modesty?

**A** I address modesty from my point of view in chapter two. What do the fellows I have gathered think about it?

Here are some thoughts on modesty from my friend, Pastor Alan Smith:

*"There are few things more powerful than beauty. Lust is such a poor thin response to it. Lust doesn't tell us anything about the one seen. It only tells us about the ones who look, and how they look, and why. Men who lust after you have never seen you. Perhaps they've never seen anyone. Perhaps they've never seen.*

*Lustful men have asked you to dress modestly to protect them from their lust, to protect you from their lust. But if their lust isn't about you, how can what you wear affect their inward gaze? You can't cover up enough to keep lustful men from lusting or pure men from seeing beauty.*

*Men will see what they're looking for.*
*You are beautiful.*

*Modesty is not a reaction to lust. It's an expression of beauty and power. Modesty is about who you are. Modesty recognizes the sacredness of your beauty and reserves the fullness of that beauty for covenant relationship.*

*It's not about rules. It's about knowing who you are.*

*And Whose you are."*[7]

---

7 Alan Smith, *Modesty and Beauty,*

Pastor Alan has a beautiful perspective. Below you will see what the single men I interviewed also have to say.

Chad: *"Popular culture is to blame because of countless examples giving unrealistic expectations. What do you see when you look at Victoria's Secret ads? I'll tell you what you should think about: Photoshop, make-up artists, fake tans, plastic surgery, digital enhancements. Women are viewed by many men as pieces of meat. 'Hot' disappears with age. "Beautiful" is ageless. And to women that chase "beauty," thank you. Thank you for being classy and deserving of respect. Thank you for going against the popular culture. You give a guy hope."*

Chandler: *"I think, in a Christian dating relationship, you would be fooling yourself if you thought that you were not going to have to put extreme precautionary measures in place. Modesty is one of these measures."*

Spencer: *"When I see a girl who's dressed immodestly, I think:*
   *1. She's insecure.*
   *2. She is unaware of how guys think.*
   *3. She doesn't care."*
*(3 qualities you don't want in a girlfriend)*

Blake: *"I have read some Christian blogs by girls and it seems they hate it when people try to encourage them to dress modestly. They think it's the guy's job to have pure thoughts even with half-naked girls all around them.*

*While I do agree with that I guess, why not help out the guys as much as possible? No Christian guy looks at a girl that dresses immodestly and thinks, I want to date that girl."*

Warren: *"I think girls should dress in a way that inspires respect and reflects their personality. Otherwise, if they want to be valued as an object, then dress in a manner that makes them appear as a collection of body parts."*

Austin: *"The type of animal you get depends on the type of bait you put out. What kind of man will you attract by your intelligence or spiritual maturity, your wit, your loving nature, or your generosity? What kind of man will you attract by your ability to dress sexually? If you hand out what is sacred to every passerby, then the men of Christ seeking intimacy with the most sacred parts of you will be less inclined to pursue you. So what I'm saying is that how a person dresses has a big impact on how that person will be perceived."*

Wes: *"I honestly think Christian girls stress too much about how modestly they dress and don't put enough weight behind how modestly they act. Granted, it's probably not a good idea to dress without a care in the world about what's showing. Yet, modesty is more about confidence and not feeling a need to show off. That's far more important than how long or short the shorts are."*

There is nothing shameful about our bodies. Adam and Eve were naked before the fall. God was good with that. Sin came, and Adam and Eve covered their nakedness and hid. Jesus came to restore what was broken, and by faith in Christ, we have been redeemed from the curse of sin. So should we drop the fig leaf and all walk around naked now? Let me attempt to answer this.

I love watching volleyball, "Dancing With the Stars", and "So You Think You Can Dance." The costumes, particularly in the last two I mentioned, are pretty skimpy. However, as a woman I often find them beautiful and they in no way tempt me to sin. But after reading the comments from the guys, immodesty seems to be a different challenge for some men. Let's consider lovingly keeping temptation in mind for our fellow male believers as we dress.

I Corinthians 10:23-24 puts it this way: "Looking at it one way, you could say, 'Anything goes. Because of God's immense generosity and grace, we don't have to dissect and scrutinize every action to see if it will pass muster.' But the point is not to just get by. We want to live well, but our foremost efforts should be to help others live well" (The Message).

I think you are free to dress however you like. But, how do you want to steward that freedom? How about at least considering making choices out of love for your brothers (1 Corinthians 8:9)? In light of this, we certainly need the Spirit to guide us in how we dress our bodies, so let's get dressed under the influence of the Spirit.

Lord Jesus, will you help us girls walk in freedom, with wisdom and love as we choose how we dress our bodies? We really do love our brothers in Christ. Help us to consider them as we dress.

**Q** How should a girl act if she likes a guy?

**A** Jared: "If a girl likes a guy, she shouldn't have to feel like she is bound in a prison of her own emotions until he slightly gets the hint that she is into him. I mean, come on…we live in the 21st century. Flirt with him! I've always appreciated a girl who has enough confidence to put herself out there, even if I didn't feel the same way."

Michael: *"Be yourself. Cannot tell you how many times where I have begun to talk to a girl and she begins to change the way she presents herself to accommodate what she "thinks" I like in a girl. It is quite the turnoff and kills it for me."*

John: *"Making an effort not to avoid the guy is important. I see so often in girls who like a guy that they are too nervous to actually talk to him and thus the guy sees that as a sign to stay away because she doesn't like him. Have casual conversations, serve, be gentle, and he might start getting a clue."*

**Q** What do you think girls need to know in general about guys?

**A** Wes: "We're slow to learn sometimes, so please be patient. We aren't ever as strong or put together as we may pretend to be, so bear with us. We may just be worth it."

Michael: *"We can be dumb. We can be insensitive and most of all we are broken. So do not be surprised if the guy messes up."*

Jared: *"Guys are not going to fulfill the empty place girls have in their hearts. Many girls go looking for a guy because they are lonely or feel incomplete. Do not put us in the position to meet that need when only Christ can do that. If you look to us to be the answer, we will fail you…miserably."*

Matthew: *"Things that can really tear us down include making fun of us in front of our friends and always wanting to do things your way. Instead, sometimes, just let us take the reins on the little things. It makes us feel manly. Also, guys need a supporter/team player."*

Chad: *"We all don't meet the stereotype many girls might have about guys. There are good guys out there."*

**Q** How do guys perceive flirting?

**A** Warren: "Flirting can be words, smiles, or looks."

 Michael: *"I believe there are different types of flirting. Not to oversimplify, but two examples would be the kind where you are trying to find out more about the person's heart, their faith, and things about them. Then there is the kind of flirting where you just want to make-out."*

Flirting is a form of communication. To me, it is showing playful interest in another person. Listening, smiling, and enjoying can all be part of flirting. I love romance with my husband. It is really important in any marriage. I want my adult kids to be free in their future marriages to flirt with their spouses. I don't mind Josh and Caroline practicing non-sensual flirting as they test relationships for possibilities. My advice: be thoughtful, careful, and honest as you show interest in another person. Save your sexual flirting for your wedding night and beyond!

**Q** How important is physical attraction, including weight?

**A** Attraction is very important! Sometimes it takes time to figure that out. But in the end, if you are not physically attracted to a guy, then he is definitely not the one for you. I am still very attracted to Bruce.

In general, most boys are highly visual. God made them that way. The first time Adam saw Eve, I imagine he was pretty excited and he let God know it (Genesis 2:23).

Jared: *"When talking to guys, physical attraction is always going to be on our top list of priorities. I say this knowing that some people might jump to the conclusion that I'm shallow, but it has nothing to do with unrealistic and twisted standards of perfection. We just want to be attracted to them!"*

Chad: *"I'm not scared to admit that there have been times where I've been interested in girls solely based on their looks. Want to know how many times that has worked out for me? Well, I'm single. I can tell you that I'm not currently looking for a girl based solely on looks. It's based largely on her inner beauty. I want a woman I find just as beautiful in sweat pants, a t-shirt, no make-up, and her hair up as I do in a fancy dress and high-heels."*

Michael: *"Physical attraction does matter, but the extent to which is it important is up to you and your significant other. It is so sad to see friends' relationships based almost entirely on physical attraction. I bet you know how long those two last together, usually not too long."*

Josh: *"I'm going to notice a pretty girl. I don't mean make-up; I'm not into that. I like to see a girl's face the way God made it. Not all guys are like this, but I also like style and creativity in the way she dresses. I'm attracted to that."*

Chandler: *"I would rename it 'fitness,' not weight. Weight can be in a range, but fitness is very important to me."*

Barrett: *"I do want a woman who who takes care of her body."*

My turn now. I come from a family who has always struggled with being overweight. Bruce always laughs because when he went to my parent's house for the first time, I showed him my special diet-food shelf in our home pantry. No one was allowed to touch it without me freaking-out, and they really didn't want to anyway. It's funny, until you realize I had an all-consuming fear of being fat most of my life.

I don't ever remember *not* being conscious of what I weighed. It started a cycle of dieting in fifth grade. One hilarious and dangerous diet I tried with my friend Paige was called "I only eat apples." Yes, only apples for a whole week. I don't recommend it. In high school, I developed an eating disorder, bulimia. I know what it feels like to be tormented in the area of food and body image. Thankfully, I stopped the behavior when one of my best friends, Judy, walked in on me throwing up. I was so embarrassed. I was still super messed up in my mind for years even after I stopped purging.

My experience with an eating disorder played into Bruce's and my early years of marriage. I was obsessed with everything I ate and how much exercise I was logging. I had a strong belief that my attractiveness was directly connected to my weight. In my mind, I didn't deserve to be seen as desirable, unless I was *very* thin. Picture that time in my life as me being a slave to food, exercise, and my fears. It took me years to believe that I'm free from sin (Romans 6:18) and to learn the art of walking in the Spirit when it comes to food and body image. I have not "arrived" and there are days I might begin to slip into a slight "fear" about my body. However, I have generally been walking in deep freedom for a long time now. It is soooo good. Food is not my enemy; it is a blessing (1 Timothy 6:17).

Want to hear my theory? I estimate that there is about a ten to fifteen pound range of healthiness for each individual person in between two ranges of weight for their height and body type. Let me clarify what I mean by this. If you are trying to be thinner than what is healthy for your body, you become a slave to food by denying yourself. Most likely, you will be thinking about food all the time. It has become an idol. You might even be hurting your body by starving yourself to distraction.

Now let's move beyond the heavier side of that ten-fifteen pound range of what is healthy for your height and body type. You might be slipping into overeating. Being overweight is not God's heart for you. Gluttony is another sin like getting drunk or stealing (Proverbs 23:20-21; Philippians 3:19). You can become a slave to food by gluttonous behavior. We are not made for sin. We are free from its power. No one makes you starve yourself or put that extra bite in your mouth. If this is a struggle for you, get some professional help. Food is meant to be a blessing. Your body is a temple that you get to take care of (1 Corinthians 6:19-20). You are in control and get to decide what weight you are comfortable with. I would love to be thinner, but I choose to have an occasional glass of wine and enjoy dark chocolate. That is the decision I have made for this season. By the Spirit and His fruit of self-control that lives in me, my body has gently landed where it is, based on my choices.

Our daughter, Caroline was recently feeling stress over all the delicious food she ate on her "study abroad" experience in Oxford, England. Like most women I know, she is tempted to get discouraged in the area of her weight. Sensing her concern, I sent her this text just last night;

*"Body/Food/Choices*
*Your identity is not tied to your season in Oxford.*
*Nor is it tied to a high school girl you once were.*
*The reality is...*
*that each day/each moment is its own.*
*Your future is free from your past.*
*And you are powerful/free/equipped to steward your*
*body in wise/loving ways ...*
*Each day is its own.*
*Walk in freedom, child of God."* 🖤

Like I said before, many men are highly visual by design. God made them that way. When you are married, your body is not just yours (1 Corinthians 7:4). You are sharing it with your man. It is respectful to take care of yourself.

However, our hope cannot be placed in this aging temple. Looks are deceiving and will fade (Proverbs 31:30). If your mate was in some sort of accident and became disfigured, how would you respond? How would you want him to respond if that happened to you? Our bodies are fragile, so it is not wise to put our hope in beauty. Girls, look out there. You see all kinds of couples with different looks, shapes, and sizes. Some of my friends with the best romantic lives are not Mr. and Mrs. Body Builder. I also know people with almost perfect physiques who don't have much physical intimacy. Trust me, you would be surprised.

Pursue healthiness throughout your life, but know that it is not all that matters. Relax. Lord willing, you will attract a boy who is attracted to you by God's design.
For more help: www.focusonthefamily.com/lifechallenges/abuse-and-addiction/eating-disorders/eating-disorders

## Q Can we discuss making-out?

A Making-out—what a vague term. It must mean more than a kiss on the cheek or holding hands. Does it mean just kissing this month, but moving on to groping hands the next month? Does it imply prepping your body for sex, but not following through?

## Here is what a few of the guys had to say.

Brandt: *"I don't think that it is wrong in itself. But it can be very dangerous. It creates strong emotional and physical ties with someone you may not marry. It can very easily lead to more physicality, no matter how strong you think you are to temptation."*

Michael: *"It can be a slippery slope because you might think, it is harmless, but I've learned that this passion can lead you both to a place neither of you should go. Easier said than done, I confess."*

Jared: *"If you have no peace about any physical act you take part in, you should stop, even if that is holding hands. However, I don't like to make blanket statements or rules on things that aren't specifically discussed in Scripture."*

Wes: *"I think that in principle there is nothing wrong with showing your affection through making-out while dating. But if the relationship deteriorates to being solely based on physical affection, then I think there's a problem. But the problem would be the shallowness of the relationship, not the making-out. I don't think that making out has to lead to anything else (a kind of "gateway drug" theory)."*

Josh: *"This is something I have thought about for a really long time. It's strange being a Christian and living in this culture. Making-out is all around us on film and TV and it's seen as a coming-of-age experience or a rite of passage. I know actions always have cause and effect.... no matter what it is....if you make out all night...you're more likely to mess up.....Is it a sin? I don't know....Do I feel guilty?  How much guilt is from the Holy Spirit, and how much comes from the messages we hear in church or from our parents? I think a lot of physicality is like a*

*swimming pool. There is a shallow end and a deep end.
I don't know where the middle ground is. Some people
get close to the deep end on their tippy-toes so, it's nice
to have guidelines beforehand."*

This last young man is my son. Notice the guys don't all
agree on these topics. I'm showing you different perspectives
on purpose, because this is an opportunity for you to ask God
what real love looks like. Girls, I told you what I think about
this topic in chapter two. Remember, I'm not into a list of rules.
I hope to encourage Spirit-led guidelines to keep you safe
both emotionally and physically. Have you thought about what
it does to the guy when he gets so aroused? By making-out,
you are contributing to putting him in a position where the
temptation for him to sin increases, including when he is alone
in his bedroom. Is that real love as his sister in Christ? Good
decisions can keep you and the guy you're with from being
tormented by the enemy of your soul as you steward your
sexuality. I hope loving guidelines will keep you from kissing
a boy in a way that preps his and your body for sex. That is
not for you…yet. Sexual activity is perfectly designed for the
marriage covenant. Someday, I hope you make-out often with
your husband. I'm so into that.

**Q** What lines might a guy try on a girl he is trying be sexual with?

**A** Adam: "I would venture to say that more than a line, a guy would, over a period of time try to push the boundaries a little further each time the couple is intimate. Of course lines like, 'oh, come on,' or 'it's not a big deal' can be used. A different tactic could be pushing a girl further than she is willing to go sexually, and once she turns the boy down, trying to do something that seems less intense, and potentially guilt the girl into thinking she should do the 'lesser' act."

 *Robin:*
*"If you really love me, you'll..."*
*"I guess you're not as committed to our relationship as I am."*
*"It's not a big deal."*
*"I just see our relationship ending in marriage."*

One of my husband's best friends, Steve, says, "If a guy does not hold the girl in enough honor and respect to not push the physical side on her, then the relationship is not worth keeping. Be assured that if he puts her in that position now, he will do it in the future – not just with sex, but with other aspects of life as well: money, family, friends, all to manipulate the relationship to get what he wants."

**Q** What do you think about guys and porn?

**A** Chad: "When I was younger, I looked at porn, but honestly haven't looked at it in years. Guys find comfort in it, but that is a dark place. It can be very addictive. It detaches guys from reality because it is fake. I'm focused on finding something real. Emotional satisfaction is far more important to me now."

*Michael: "Almost every guy my age I have known has had some run-in with pornography, one way or another. It can be a very addictive thing and I went through a dark period with it during middle school and into high school. It affected my relationships with girls and it has been something I still have to fight the urge to go back to. A pivotal change started when my faith became more important to me because I found myself so lost and broken. If a guy you're interested in has a problem, you need to hold off. I'm not saying he can't ever be dateable, but at that point, he is not ready for a relationship."*

Remember chapter two and the question: "So I have been sexual, how do I have a redo?" In that chapter, I tell the story of the night my husband was out of town. That evening our then high school daughter felt led to expose the story occurring between her and a boyfriend. I promised to tell you the second half of the story that involved her then-high-school-senior brother, Josh. I have his heartfelt blessing to share it.

During the fall of his senior year, our son had been coming home mysteriously late every Thursday night since school started. This meant he was skipping the dinner that I made him. When he got home one evening I dramatically said, "I have had it!" (You know, in that "mom" tone.)

Later that evening, I was in our daughter's room. In the middle of Caroline's confessions, she slipped out of her room to put her clothes in the dryer. At that very moment, Josh walked into her room, not knowing what she had just shared with me. He sat down right next to me on the edge of her bed. Quickly and gently he leaned close to my ear and said, "Mom, the reason I'm never home on Thursday nights is because I'm meeting with Austin at Chipotle to eat and talk. I used to have a masturbation problem and he has been praying with me and walking me through it. I haven't struggled with it one single time this entire school school year."

Right after the words "school year" came out of his mouth, Caroline returned into the room, like she was in a play and her cue for re-entrance had been spoken. Josh stood up like clockwork, exited, and Caroline continued to confess her story about the boy she had been dating. Neither sibling had any idea that they had each decided to reveal hidden truths to their mom on that particular night.

After both kids were settled in their rooms, I went straight outside to discuss all of this with God and make a phone call to Bruce. Although, I took seriously each child's confession, I couldn't help but laugh. Where was Bruce? Was there a "confession memo" that I missed?

As the weeks rolled on, Josh continued to open up to both Bruce and me about his past struggle. Turns out, porn played a large role in his battle. He described years of being enslaved by it. There were nights he spent on his knees crying for God to help him overcome his sinful behavior.

We had no idea . . .

Crazy thing was, Josh felt great once the truth was out. He was walking in freedom and was so happy to be "known" by his mom and dad. This was new information to us, information I needed to process with God. I felt no shame or condemnation for my son. Trust me, with my sin track record, I'm a much-forgiven woman. I am very certain about the grace of God. I'm very sure of His love. I'm outright confident our sins were completely taken care of on the cross. All of that not only applies to me, but to my son.

But, I'm a mom. This is my only son. I was hurting for the past, wrestling with the thought of having a tormented boy right under our family roof and not knowing it. Eventually, after a few weeks when I had the full story, I found myself alone one evening. There I was, on our laundry room floor, for a long time crying to God like a little baby. I was profoundly grieved. Could I have done anything different? Our son had been silently suffering all those years.

I began to put the pieces together. Things started making sense. I realized the time-frame of his struggle directly coincided with Josh's pushing his sister and me away emotionally and physically. At the time, you could forget trying to hug him or sit close to him. He used frustration and anger to keep us away. Looking back, I can imagine that keeping a secret that involves objectifying women does not make you want to gravitate towards your mom and your sister.

**1 in 5 mobile searches are for pornography
68 percent of young adult men and 18 percent of
women use porn at least once every week.**

**64 percent of Christian men and 15 percent
of Christian women say they watch porn
at least once a month.[8]**

Josh is so cool. He is confident in his freedom in Christ and in his paid-for forgiveness. He has no shame. Today, he is actually the most open person I have ever met on the taboo subject of porn and masturbation. As the Lord leads, he is happy to help others find freedom when he can. Perhaps, this is because he felt so helpless for so many years. His guy friends come to him often for advice and prayer. Several of our friends with younger sons have come to Josh for counsel on how they can help their young men.

So how does a guy who is into porn affect you, my dear? Profoundly. Porn can actually mess with their brains. "Cambridge University researchers found that compulsive porn users react to porn cues in the same way that drug addicts react to drug cues."[9] Pornography is not harmless or normal. It is a secret sin. Don't assume it will stop when guys get married. If you want an intimate marriage, forget secrets. If I had a USB cord, I would hook it up to our brains and replay for you the damage I have seen porn cause in marriages. Porn and the masturbation that accompanies it has cost some women their

8  Pure Desire Ministries www.puredesire.org.
9  Cambridge Study: *Internet porn addiction mirrors drug addiction* (2014).

entire sex lives with their husbands. Because of it, some men don't even desire their own wives and end up having sexless marriages. A guy who is into porn has no need for his wife. That type of rejection causes so much pain to women I have known. I have seen it contribute to affairs. Or it can lead guys to being super sexually demented and weird with their wives. Yuck. And, who wants to be compared to another woman merely pretending in a porn video?

Healthy, loving, unashamed godly sex is what you want. Not all guys are into porn. Girls, don't settle for less.

There is good news for sinners and porn users. Jesus loves them, hangs out with them, and intimately shares meals with sinners of all kinds (Mark 2:15-17). If this is your issue, this is no way to live. Looking at pornographic images does not prepare you for a healthy unashamed marriage and future sex life. Porn will never satisfy you. Jesus is the ultimate source of satisfaction. Both guys and girls can overcome a porn pattern in their lives. Josh did. God is not mad at you (Romans 5:9). You do not have to be a slave to lust (Romans 6:12-14). You have everything you need for *life* and godliness (2 Peter 1:3). Satan loves secrets (Ephesians 6:12). If porn is a problem for you, get some help. Find someone like Josh did to confess to and pray with. Live in the freedom and shamelessness that belongs to you as a child of God (James 5:16; Ephesians 5:13-16).

In John 8:36 Jesus said, "I tell you most solemnly that anyone who chooses a life of sin is trapped in a dead-end life and is, in fact, a slave. A slave is a transient, who can't come and go at will. The Son, though, has an established position, the run of the house. So if the Son sets you free, you are free through and through" (The Message).

# unashamed

# chapter four

# what ever happened to dating?

Clearly, I have dated a lot of guys in my day. I had my first
boyfriend when I was in fourth grade. Imagine a social life
without texting. We experienced minimal physical interaction
by passing scribbled notes on paper or verbal messages
through friends. I had another boyfriend in junior high who
kept giving me sheets of folded notebook papers, asking me
to meet him behind the gym after school to make out. What
is funny is that I didn't really know what making out meant.
So, I kept avoiding his offers. I also remember a late night
slumber party in junior high where we discussed dating. We
wanted to be prepared. What if a boy decided to try and kiss
us goodnight? It was determined by group consensus that
we better practice by kissing our pillows. And yes, we actually
kissed our pillows. Luckily there was no Instagram or Snapchat.

Fast forward to Bruce's and my two adult children in
their 20's, Josh and Caroline. The topic of dating is of great
interest to both of them and their friends. Lots of texting,

e-mailing, and late night talks have gone into my thoughts on this subject.

## Q What ever happened to dating?

A I got my undergraduate degree from the University of Texas in Austin. While there, I remember having three dates with three different guys within one week. One of those dates was arranged by a friend who set me up with a boy I had never met. Yep, it was a "blind date." All three dates were fun and nothing profound occurred except that I got to know three guys. Does anyone even do that anymore? Anyway, there was no pressure to know if you "liked" someone or to be "official." You definitely didn't have to be exclusive to go on dates.

I'm aware, there is a wild and crazy side of dating going on out there. Bruce and I are always rolling our eyes when people in movies or on television meet on a first date and then are seen the next day waking up in the same bed. Really? I'm using all the self- control I can to not go off about how foolish, painful, and devastating casual, unmarried sex is. I addressed this in chapter two.

However, there is another side to this dating coin for many single Christian girls. The words *courtship* and *dating* are not really found in the Bible. So, what is the point? Perhaps dating is an opportunity to spend time with new people and explore the relationship. But, in the midst of my kids' Christian culture, the freedom to date around just does not seem to exist. One Christian girl told me yesterday that her biggest anxiety is what others will think of her if she dates a guy or, even worse, dated several guys. What I find with these girls is that there is tremendous pressure to be sure you "like" someone before even going on a coffee date. Many girls have been so focused and fearful of doing it all "right" and staying "pure" that they are almost paralyzed about the subject of a dating. It gets very complicated for them.

I am going to keep reminding you that you can't lose your purity by dating. Let me repeat. Christ is our "purity." His blood has made you clean (Hebrews 9:11-28). That's the Gospel. And yes, if you belong to Christ, you receive His Spirit who gives you the power to make wise choices in dating. God's Spirit leads you to love, joy, peace, self-control, and ultimately life. God never wants you to hurt yourself. Therefore, His Spirit would never lead you to sin while you explore dating. But either way, in Christ, your purity is sealed.
Okay, now that is settled.

Here is what one of my young, single girlfriends texted me: "Dating is to get to know someone, and sometimes there are qualities I don't love that are revealed. I don't want to hurt a guy's feelings. But I feel stuck. It makes me nervous to start dating someone again without knowing him first-- I'd love to be able to build a friendship first without the 'dating' title because there's less pressure that way."

See what I mean? It seems to some girls and guys that the "dating" title pushes a relationship too quickly into exclusivity before two people know each other. If a guy asked a girl out when I was in my 20's, it didn't make her off-limits to other guys, unless the two of them had mutually agreed that they wanted "boyfriend/girlfriend" status. Back then, going on dates was a means of learning, not a claim to a person. I went out with a guy for a season in college who said on our third date that he needed a very large shot of bourbon after a hard day of work. I remember thinking, *I am so OUT OF HERE!* And I was.

Or, how about another guy I got "set up" with, who, after a few dates, picked me up in a pair of 1980's red plaid golf pants? I assure you, it was our last date! At that time, dating was viewed as an opportunity to get to know someone. It provided each person a chance to see how the other one communicated, get a glimpse into their character, and find out whether they drank too much. We even discovered how they dressed (smile). No plaid pants, please.

I do not know how to change a culture. But I do know that *you* get to decide for yourself what dating means to *you*. If someone wants to get to know you, he can do it the way you are comfortable with. You get to share that with anyone you please. It is not some religious thing that you need to tiptoe around. Christ can lead you in this important area. So even though others around you might view dating one way, you get to decide how you are going to date.

**Q** What are the things that bug you about "dating" in the Christian culture??

**A** Let me offer some answers to this by sharing what a couple of my single guy friends think:

Chandler: *"There is just this unbelievable hesitancy, and it has plagued many Christian circles. I desperately wish that somehow we could reverse this idea that for dating to take place, it has to be this really careful, hesitant ordeal."*

Wes: *"The obsession with 'the one.' I hate that it sets up all this pressure, and people don't get to know each other because they're afraid that they might not want to spend the rest of their lives together."*

**Q** **Should I group date before an actual alone date with a guy?**

**A** I think that is a great idea. Anything you can do to get to know someone is probably smart. But I'm funny about "shoulds." There are no "dating rules" and certainly no "dating police."

I remember my daughter calling me from her Christian college, crazy late one night. She was wondering if it was okay that she had been alone for several late-night hours with a good guy friend practicing for an upcoming singing event. She was not even on a date. She is sort of shy and he really helped her make a breakthrough emotionally as a singer. Nothing romantic or inappropriate happened. They had a blast. However, there was this subtle, shameful sinking tone in her voice on the phone. She feared she had done something wrong. She knew she has friends who would never spend time alone with a guy late at night like she did. It was as if she had broken some imaginary rule by being alone with a guy.

I was happy to hear about her evening. I was glad for it. My kids need to loosen up a little. I am not talking about sinning. Remember, I have covered that in chapter two. But girls, if we are someday going to be married and free, fun, and spontaneous with our spouses, we need to relax a little. If you decide to date, for goodness sake have a great time. Enjoy it (1 Timothy 6:17).

Sure, you need to use common sense. Of course, you need to know the character of a guy before you put yourself in a situation where he could take advantage of you physically. For instance, being alone in a room with a closed door is not the wisest decision. That is a safety thing. But there is no rule about spending time with others, even if it's a guy, even if you're alone. You can tell when things are getting weird. You are smart. Listen to the Holy Spirit. Be safe. Get to know and enjoy your brothers in Christ. Many of them are mature and awesome.

**Q** Should he be a Christian for me to date him?

**A** Dang, I told you I don't like the word *should.* But . . . date and marry a Christian (2 Corinthians 6:14)! There, I said it. Let's stand firm on this one. It is not a rule or a law. However, it is *extremely wise.* For me, thinking of your marrying a non-Christian is like watching a little kid running in the street and wanting to rescue that little one. But you are adults and I can't see you. *Girls, don't do it!* I have never met a Christian woman, who married a nonbeliever and didn't have great sorrow and regret over that decision. If only you could hear the pain of women who have chosen men who denied Christ or vaguely resembled a "Christian" while they dated. Then they got married. Then the pain began. Then they had children and chasm became even more profound. My desire is for you to see the tears of women over the years who have shared their stories of husbands who didn't ultimately share their faith in Christ. I am not talking about judging whether he is going to a church or reading his Bible. I'm not looking for a list of performance-based rituals to prove his faith. Look for the fruit of the Spirit (Galatians 5:22-23). Every child of God is unique and experiences God in his own way. My husband experiences his faith in a way that looks very different than the way I experience mine. What matters is what the man believes. Talk about it with him. Don't assume that the young man believes like you do. Is he born again in the Spirit of Christ? Be as sure as you can about this (John 3:3-8).

One final note, I have a dear friend who did not know Christ and the man she was dating led her to Christ. This man is now her husband. There are always exceptions. However, I encourage you to date a believer, but in the end you must listen to the Spirit of God.

There is an unspoken code that girls have with their girlfriends. Here is how it works. We talk about a guy a lot. (Often he has no idea this is happening). Since we have a "crush" on him, our friends are not even allowed to get to know the guy. Sorry, we called dibs first. This "code" closes a door for other girls to like the same guy, just because we beat them to the punch. Girls, may I suggest that it is not fair to the guy, or to your friends. He might be better suited for your other girlfriend. I know this is hard. Try not to be possessive of your brothers in Christ unless you are truly in a mutually

exclusive relationship. You can trust God to let everyone get to
know each other and let the Spirit move.

I just broke code…

**Q** Should I go on a date with any guy who asks
me, or only with those I could see myself actually
marrying?

**A** My opinion is to be open. Sometimes you can't really
know if a new relationship is going to go well until you
try it. So, consider going, and be open to having a good time.
Even if you don't end up continuing the dating process with
this particular person, you can always become friends.

If there is *no way* you could ever see yourself with him,
then feel free to gracefully say no. You don't have to go on
a date with anyone you don't think you would want to have
a relationship with. But ladies, let's be kind in the way we
communicate. It takes some guys a lot of courage to ask a
girl out.

**Q** How should a guy act on a date?

**A** There is that word *should* again. There are no real
"shoulds." But here are a few observations to ponder.
Take notice if your date talks mostly about himself. Does he
ask you questions about your life? Does he listen? If you are
shy, you won't mind if he does most of the talking. However, I
like a well-balanced interaction.

I consider my sister, Jean, an expert on etiquette. Here is one of her thoughts: "It's important for a date to make plans and keep them! Guys shouldn't be characterized by waiting until the last minute to ask a girl out."

Here is the opinion of Chad, an awesome, single, Christian man in his late twenties: "I'm a big believer that chivalry isn't dead. Gentlemen open doors, pull out the chairs, *pay the check,* walk a lady on the inside of the street."

Some of these behaviors are "southern" ways of thinking. I have to confess: I like them. I think as believers, we should respect and honor each other. These are just some ways that guys can show honor and care toward the girls they date. It's okay if your opinion is different than mine on this. If a dating relationship continues, at some point I encourage you to communicate with the guy about what is important to you.

## Q What about drinking and dating?

A Adam: "Drinking and dating are not a healthy pair. There's a lot of pressure to do both simultaneously. I have undoubtedly been a part of more fights when fueled by alcohol than when I haven't had anything to drink. Alcohol clouds judgment, whether it's driving a car or making bad decisions sexually."

Drinking is a personal matter for you to work out with God. In answering this question, I'm going to keep my thoughts on how it relates to dating. In my opinion, drinking alcohol, or smoking pot for that matter, is not a good idea while dating. Err on the side of caution. God wants you to be safe. I have one particular story, which I'm more than glad to forget. It happened on a college night when I probably made one of the worst decisions I have ever made. It involved my drinking too much and an old boyfriend. It didn't end well. God forgave it on the cross and remembers it no more, so I am agreeing with Him. But for your sake, I bring it up because I would counsel you to not drink and date.

If you have reached the legal age for drinking and choose to have a glass of alcohol responsibly, consider saving it for a time with your girlfriends, a wedding, your family or when you get married. Some day, I think it would be wonderful for your husband to take advantage of you as you share a glass of wine (wink). Remember, Jesus drank wine (John 2:1-11), but never got drunk. It's as foolish as overeating or stealing. We have self-control. Don't ever become a slave to things that were designed to be a blessing to you (2 Peter 1:3; Ecclesiastes 9:7; Ephesians 5:18; 1 Timothy 5:23; Romans 14:20-23; Galatians 5:19-21; 1 Corinthians 6:12).

**Q** **Does the guy need to lead and be the pursuer in the relationship?**

**A** First of all, remember no one is your husband until he is your husband. When you see verses talking about a husband's role reflecting Christ, such as 1 Corinthians 11:3, the head of the church, remember that idea does not apply unless you are married, However, while dating you can observe a guy's behavior for clues to the kind of man you're interested in marrying. Every relationship is made up of two unique individuals coming together. My husband is a manly man and hard worker. But in personal relationships, he is laid back, while I'm full of many ideas and lots of initiative, by God's design. We have a great relationship and we submit mutually to each other, especially when the one of us is more gifted in one area than the other. We don't have any super-defined "roles" or "rules" on who initiates in our relationship. Yes, Bruce leads our family. But Bruce is organic in his approach to leadership. He walks in the Spirit. He demonstrates his strengths as he leads, and when needed, he encourages me in leading areas that are good for our family as well (Ephesians 5:21).

In the realm of dating, what concerns me is a girl who is desperate for love, affection, or attention. It is unhealthy for a woman to keep pursuing and initiating a relationship out of insecurity or trying to capture a guy. I like a lot of interaction and interest from my man. What if the guy isn't responding much because he is super-passive in general, or worse, doesn't really want to pursue that particular girl? You never want to be convenient. You want to be his highly desired choice. I never want you to appear easy, desperate, pushy, or needy. Personally, I wouldn't want to have to "work" too hard for some passive guy. We deserve better than that, girls. Don't make excuses to justify a relationship. You are not that needy. Learn to be content in Christ. Focus on God, your girlfriends, and developing new relationships. If a guy isn't giving you enough attention, move on.

**Q** Who should pay when I'm on a date?

**A** I will show you two separate views on this:

 Adam: *"It can be emasculating to some men for a woman to pay for a date. However, most young adults don't have a ton of disposable income. I think anyone who has dated a significant other for an extended period of time would agree: offer to pay."*

 Mitch: *"Dating is nothing more than two individuals spending time together. There is no eternal connection. Our society tells us that it is chivalrous to pay for your lady, and I concede that the guy should pay on occasion as there is no sense marrying someone you won't spend money on. But it is ridiculous to place the responsibility to pay on someone just because they have a Y chromosome."*

My turn, I tried to be considerate of the guys I dated and found creative ways to share the load financially. I'm from Texas, you know, so southern ways are definitely part of my upbringing. Honestly, I found a guy who wanted to pay for me to be very charming and fitting with what I would be eventually looking for in a husband. I always wanted to be a stay-at-home wife and mother, so, I loved it when a guy wanted to pay. Just keeping it real, ladies. But Mitch is right, you are not married until you are married, and these guys deserve some financial consideration. A single lady-friend of mine says that she knows lots of single women who think this way: "I really want him to offer to pay because that's the gentlemanly thing to do. However, I want to pay my own way on the first date and maybe a few dates thereafter because then there is *no feeling of obligation.*" She believes it's much cleaner relationally when each person pays his or her own way until both are agreed that the relationship needs to go to another level. It keeps things on a friendship level instead of a dating level—until it's time to move into a real dating relationship. I believe her point of view is a valid one for you to consider.

**Q** **How do you think social media affects dating?**

**A** In this device-driven culture, there is a temptation to pre-judge the character of a guy before having really spent any significant time interacting with him in person. I believe social media plays a large role in this discussion. I think social media is a powerful tool and can be used for lots of good--and for bad. However, let's ponder how it affects the foundation of our face-to-face relationships. Dating, in person, allows us to observe nuances in social cues. Body language is important. Details such as eye contact, smiling, and the ability to sense if the conversation needs to move in a different direction are crucial.

Blake Eastman, body language expert and founder of The Nonverbal Group says:

> "*People have an easier time picking out an emoticon to display the emotion they are feeling rather than actually showing it on their face. Unfortunately, for*

*the past 10 years, people have been really confident behind the computer keyboard, but then you see them in person and things are very different."*[10]

Alone, in front of our screens, we often *think* we discover so much about a person from Facebook-stalking, Instagram, and texting before we ever get to know them. A real human is always more complex than written words, a profile, or a series of pictures.

**Q** What are your thoughts on texting and dating?

**A** I enjoy all forms of communication in my relationship with Bruce. Texting is a fantastic one. My son, Josh, and my young friend, Kayla, both say that a lot of texting is probably *not* a great tool to *start* a relationship. They claim it should not be the main source of getting to know someone until the relationship is further along. I think this is wise advice.

Recent college graduate, Emmy, says that girls sometimes "hide behind texting and are too available to guys." I agree with her. I don't want my daughter to feel obligated to be available to a guy 24/7. That seems a little invasive to me. Let's show some thoughtful boundaries and restraint in our texting. After all, we have self-control. If a guy wants to get to know you, I encourage you to connect more often with face-to-face contact (Proverbs 25:28; Galatians 5:22-23).

---

10 Ashley Strickland, *The lost art of offline dating.*

**Q** How much should I communicate with a guy while dating?

**A** Adam: "We aren't telepathic. Communication is key. I think that telling a guy your feelings, straight up, can help solve many problems."

In my most important relationships, I'm going for intimacy. This means to "know" the other person and be "known" by them. I don't enjoy being super-self conscious, with thoughts like, *Should I say this?* I just want to relax and be myself. I desired to be as comfortable with my future spouse as I was with my best friend. So I really believe prayer is the answer here. Talk with God as you are getting to know a guy. God knows the best timing and when to open up about what is on your mind and heart. If you feel prompted to share something, pray, and see if you have peace about it (Colossians 3:15). However, if you often feel you "can't" say things to the guy you are dating, I would question whether he is the right one for you.

**Q** How do I know if I have a real connection with a guy or if I'm just excited about a new thing?

**A** Good question. It's fun to be excited about a person. First of all, the connection needs to be mutual. If it is, then go ahead and spend a little time with him. However, I would not make myself always available at all hours, including through social media. I suggest you go though all four seasons of the year with a guy before you make any major decisions. Time is a pretty good indicator. However, remember God's ways are sometimes not like ours (Isaiah 55:8). You meet some couples who "know" they have met the person they want to marry right away. Bruce and I did, but even then, we dated for a while before getting engaged.

**Q** What is "guarding my heart" and does it even pertain to dating?

**A** Here is the verse this young woman is referring to: "Watch over your heart with all diligence, for from it flow the springs of life" (Proverbs 4:23, NASB).

Guarding your heart is a dance between two places. Picture two young women, one is so hungry for love she is quick to attach herself to a guy before she has much information about him. She makes compromises sexually before he is committed to her for the long haul. When that doesn't work, she is quickly off and onto another guy. There is a sense that this girl has an emotional need she is trying to fill with a man.

Now picture another girl with a different approach. She is so timid and afraid that she keeps her heart under lock-and-key, so much so, that some guys won't even come near her. She is so inwardly focused that she probably has a hard time attracting guys or at least building a warm relationship that could lead to an intimate partnership one day. Each girl, in each case, is set up for relational sorrow.

Guys struggle with this too.

 Chad: *I find myself emotionally diving in head-first far too often in relationships. Yet, if you guard your heart too long and don't open up, the relationship cannot grow, which means you won't find out if the relationship is real."*

Some are worried that there might be emotional boundaries they shouldn't cross. This is a double-sided coin. On one side, some level of healthy vulnerability is attractive and helpful in the discovery process of dating. I would say you have to be willing to feel awkward or, even worse, be hurt, if you are going to open yourself up to connect with another person. Emotions are not bad and you will survive if you have pain. The Holy Spirit is really good at comforting us when we need it. On the flip side of that same coin, it is wise to guard your heart as you explore relationships. This means being careful about the character of the guy you are dating. Among other things, it means not assuming anything and not daydreaming too much about the future with a guy.

Adam: *"The word love can be devalued quickly the more often you use it. The closer you keep your heart, the more a guy has to work for your admiration and affection. Being with the right guy that will do that is worth it once you find him."*

"Guarding your heart" also means not being a one-sided-pursuer-girl. Don't "work" to keep the relationship going. It means being willing to walk away if you do not have peace or if he is not giving you a healthy amount of attention. It also means not getting involved sexually. Because let's face it, ladies, our sexuality and heart are deeply intertwined.

And so, you may wonder, what if I did get sexually involved? What do I do with my heart then?

Well, I would say that you definitely didn't guard your heart, in that case. First, you owe yourself an apology. The least you can do is deeply and completely forgive yourself. Since Christ has forgiven you for everything you have *ever* done, who are you to judge yourself? If He says you are forgiven and it is forgotten, agree with Him. The Holy Spirit wants to comfort you and remind you that God is still close to you and that you are clean. Let your heart believe that. You will start to experience some deep mending and freedom. You can breathe again. You can start fresh (Colossians 3:13; 1 Corinthians 4:3; 2 Corinthians 5:17, 21; Psalm 103:12).

So, I say, join the dance. Trust Jesus to keep your heart safe and partner with Him as He gently leads you in the discovery process in dating. Be open, careful, and keep talking to your God as you venture out in getting to know the men He created.

**Q** **How do I handle difficult conversations or conflict with my boyfriend?**

**A** Often times, conflicts arise out of our unfulfilled desires. Author Anne Lamott says, "Expectations are resentment waiting to happen."[11]

I am a great lover of *freedom*. I really don't like anyone telling me what to do. If I find myself in a relationship where I sense someone is judging me, wanting to take from me, or trying to control me in any way, you will often find me gently distancing myself. I try and extend my respect for freedom to others.

When my traveling husband signed up for three softball teams in the early days of our marriage, I was pretty sad, frustrated, and disappointed. I remember approaching

---

11 Anne Lamott. *Crooked Little Heart.*

him about the subject. However, when I told him of my sorrow over his choice, I had no expectation that he would quit. Most importantly, I just wanted to be known by him. So, I remember acknowledging that he was an adult and could do whatever he wanted. But, I let him know how his choice was affecting the kids and me. The cool thing is he would never do that now. He would tell you himself that he was being foolish and selfish. You see, God begins a good work in each of us, including my husband (Philippians 1:6). At the time, my lack of expectations allowed me to get what I ultimately wanted more than I wanted him home—I wanted intimacy and to be known. I have control over my husband's knowing me and knowing my heart. By communicating, without expectation or judgment, it made a difficult situation bearable. Yet, notice I did not get everything I wanted. In the end, I respected Bruce's freedom because I knew it was God's job to change Bruce's heart, not mine. Sure enough over time, the Lord did just that.

Here is what I have learned about boys and men, in general. My son and husband both do better if I can consolidate my thoughts. I probably use three times more words when I talk about the same subject with my girlfriends. It is a brain thing. I like to be heard, and I've learned that I can increase my chances of really being heard if I exercise a little self-control. Both of my men, Bruce and our son Josh, start to daydream if I get long-winded.

Bruce and I have learned a great communication tool for dealing with conflict with someone from our counselor and friend, Leah Springer:

1. *This is what I have seen/witnessed (facts, unemotional)...*

2. *When I observe this it makes me think...*

3. *When I think that, it makes me feel...*

4. *My hope would be...*

Give this tool a try next time you want to discuss a difficult subject in a relationship.

Adam: *"If you don't talk to your boyfriend then he's not going to know what is bothering you or what he should do differently. Listen to what he has to say, and tell him how you feel. If he makes good points don't be afraid to admit it, but if this is something that truly bothers you, tell him."*

**Q** **My parents don't really like the guy I am dating. Does that even matter?**

**A** Yes, it does. What should you do about their not liking him? It depends on what the guy is like and what your parents are like. Do your parents know Jesus? Why don't you think they like this guy? Are their concerns legitimate? Are you being respectful to your parents and calmly validating their caution? Is the guy willing to spend time with them? Ask God for wisdom (James 1:5). If your parents are believers, consider praying with them about the situation. Sometimes your family can see things that you don't.

**Q** If you are dating someone that has a wild past,
should that cause distrust in the relationship now?

**A** I'm not going to lie… Bruce and I were each pretty
promiscuous before we met, so much so that it ended
up affecting our marriage greatly in the early years. But we
were not Christians. So, I think it's a little different when you
are dealing with two believers who are dating. Here is what
I think. I would be very suspicious of a guy who is currently
super-promiscuous, who says he is a Christian. I am not
questioning his salvation, but I would wonder how intimately
he walks in the freedom from the power of sin that Christ
has purchased for him (Romans 6:18). I would be concerned
about how much he values Scripture's wisdom, and have to
ask whether he gives himself a "hall-pass" for sexual activity.
That guy concerns me because I wonder if he would eventually
cheat on you.

I have a son and I tell him that wet dreams are God's
gift to boys. No shame in them. I have a younger girl friend
who dated a guy that claimed he needed a sexual outlet so
badly that he allowed himself to do what he wanted in that
area with porn and girls. He believed the lie that he "needed"
release. And it appeared that it was okay with him for any
girlfriend to provide that. I think that is a major red flag.
However, if my daughter met a guy who had been foolish in
that area in the past, but had matured to a point where he
was really listening to God and believing in his power over sin
by the blood of Jesus, I would believe in the possibility of a
healthy relationship.

Sam: *"In my current relationship, I was the one with the wild past. Not everyone has to do this, but I shared everything. Her being able to forgive me meant the world to me."*

## Q What about an abusive guy?

## A Adam: "Don't stay with someone that treats you in a way that breaks you down. It's not good for you, and it reinforces his bad behavior."

Abuse comes in many forms: emotional, physical, mental, spiritual, or verbal abuse. None of that is okay. *Ever.* Pay attention to the smallest of signs of unhealthy behavior. For instance, do you avoid subjects out of fear of angering your partner? Does he criticize, humiliate, or yell at you? Does he ignore your thoughts, desires, and opinions? Does he blame you for his bad behavior? Does he try to control your relationships? Does he threaten to hurt you or physically abuse you? Sometimes it takes a while to find out if a guy is manipulative or unkind. Don't feel bad if you start dating a man and then later discover he is abusive. The new information you gather requires a new response. You are *never* stuck in a dating relationship. You always have a choice. No matter how hard it is. Say goodbye to this young man; he is not for you.

My dear friend, Kerrie Oles, author of *Revived*, experienced significant abuse in her past. I emailed her and asked her to answer this question:

*"Sadly, abuse affects our ability to see ourselves as God designed us. We were uniquely created in His image, and when we are abused in some way abuse distorts our perception of ourselves, but ultimately it can distort our perception of God.*

*No matter how wonderful you think this abuser is, he needs healing too. Forgiveness and moving away from this kind of relationship is never an indicator that you are lacking grace, but a sure sign that you value who you were created to be and your intimacy with your Father God."*

Chad: *"Should you keep dating an abusive guy? Never. Run. Get out. A guy who can abuse a woman is not a man at all, and they don't deserve your time, respect, or attention."*

**Q** **What are your thoughts on online dating?**

**A** I met Bruce before the social media scene exploded. So here is what my friend Victoria Rogers, author of *Finding a Man Worth Keeping*, e-mailed me about online dating.

*Be cautious, keeping yourself safe. Anyone can lie at any time. But online it is much easier. Married men masquerade as singles, pedophiles lurk camouflaged as teenagers. Any of those online profiles you read could be owned by a rapist. Alarming? Yes, and it should be. But does that mean never online date? Not necessarily. Just use extreme caution.*

*Plus:*

- *Never have your home address listed online!*
- *Set up a separate email address for dating sites.*
- *Don't give too many identifying details online.*
- *Meet at a public location and drive separately.*
- *Always let someone in your life know exactly when and where you are meeting an online friend.*
- *Ask him if he is married or has been. Ask him if he has children.*
- *Ask him his view of God.*
- *Don't rush things. People can be anyone they want to be for a period of time.*

**Q** How do I break up or walk away from someone?

**A** Sometimes it takes a while to find out a relationship is not for you. Let peace be your guide (Colossians 3:15). Don't feel bad that you started dating a man, and then later discovered that he is not what you are looking for. Remember, new information you gather often requires a new response. I repeat: you are *never* stuck in a dating relationship. You always have a choice.

If you have been sexually physical in the relationship, you might find it harder to distance yourself. Girls are just made that way. Our emotions (heart) and our sexuality are very intertwined. Forgive yourself and believe that God is for you. But for goodness sake, do not stay with a boyfriend because it is difficult to leave. Do not stay in a relationship because you are scared or afraid of feeling awkward. Also, don't remain because breaking up might make you feel lonely. Don't stay with him to somehow justify the physical things you might have done in the relationship. You are free to move on. Especially if you have been physically sexual, I encourage you not to deceive yourself that you will be "friends" by just "hanging-out." That usually never works out. I have seen so many girls fall back into physical interactions with an old boyfriend and it keeps them from moving on. Plus, the next guy you date and perhaps, future husband would probably prefer that you make a clean break.

The word *break-up* has weird connotations. Because in reality, what are you "breaking up?" In marriage, the two shall become *one*. But in dating, you are *not* one. You are two separate people. You don't have to feel bad that you have changed your mind. If he is a Christian, then he is your brother in Christ, not your husband.

Lord willing, try and break off the relationship face-to-face. Be compassionate, kind, firm, and clear. Don't stall. You can do it! If he becomes creepy, needy, or disrespectful, set up some boundaries. You don't have to respond to all of his phone calls or social media attempts. As the Lord leads, you can even be silent if you need to.

Girls, you have no obligation to a man. Move on with grace.

 Adam: *"Carrying on a relationship that you know is over, but the other person does not know, is damaging. No one comes out better for having waited longer to break up."*

**Q** How do I recover from a break-up that I did not want?

**A** What you need is comfort. I know you're not a child, but I long to give you an understanding hug and say: "Oh baby girl, I'm so sorry if you're hurting." One of the Bible's most precious descriptions of the Holy Spirit is: "the Comforter (Counselor, Helper, Intercessor, Advocate, Strengthener, Standby), the Holy Spirit." (John 14:26, AMP).

As hard as being broken up with is, it is an opportunity for you to lean into God. Rest in His tender love and tune your ear to hear His voice. Jesus says, "The sheep that are My own hear and are listening to My voice; and I know them, and they follow Me" (John 10:27, AMP).

In a painful season, such as being rejected by a guy, it is extremely wise to hold your thoughts "captive." (2 Corinthians 10:5). Notice whether you are having "God thoughts" or not. Keep remembering that God will never reject you. Know that there is nothing "wrong" with you. You are not worth rejecting. This can be hard, but respect the freedom of your former boyfriend to do what he thinks is best for his life, even if he was a jerk in the way he did it. Talk it out with a trusted friend who has wisdom. Ask people to pray for you. Don't pretend. But, find ways to move on. Enjoy God. He enjoys *you.* You will heal; I promise.

# unashamed

# chapter five

# love, engagement, and marriage

**Q** How do I know if I'm in love?

**A** In the Bible the word *love* has more than one meaning, but it shows up in the English language simply as "love." However, if you look at the original Greek language of the New Testament, it actually uses more specific words to describe unique kinds of love.

*Phileo:* Think of your best friend. This is when you just can't help but be fond of someone with natural affection. Romans 12:10 uses this word: "Love one another with brotherly affection [as members of one family], giving precedence and showing honor to one another" (AMP).

*Agape:* We can agape (love) because He first loved us (1 John 4:19). This means *big love*. It is found in the New Testament more than any other of the words translated *love*. Agape describes motivation to love out of honor rather than by feelings or attraction. It is often undeserving. Consider the ability to demonstrate lavish goodness toward another person based on what is in their best interest.

1 Corinthians 13:4-7 teaches us what *agape* is:
*"Love never gives up.*
*Love cares more for others than for self.*
*Love doesn't want what it doesn't have.*
*Love doesn't strut,*
*Doesn't have a swelled head,*
*Doesn't force itself on others,*
*Isn't always "me first,"*
*Doesn't fly off the handle,*
*Doesn't keep score of the sins of others,*
*Doesn't revel when others grovel,*
*Takes pleasure in the flowering of truth,*
*Puts up with anything,*
*Trusts God always,*
*Always looks for the best,*
*Never looks back,*
*But keeps going to the end."* (The Message)

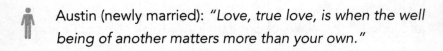 Austin (newly married): *"Love, true love, is when the well being of another matters more than your own."*

*Eros:* Is a third kind of love that refers to a physical, sensual, sexual love between a husband and wife. Check out Song of Solomon in the Bible. While the Old Testament doesn't use the word *eros,* the story in the Song of Solomon is a great example of it. When led by the Spirit, the Apostle Paul suggests that people marry to fulfill this kind of love (1 Corinthians 7:36).

 **Love and lust, what's the difference?**

**A** Spencer: "Lust seeks to get, love seeks to give. When guys are putting up boundaries, that's a good indicator of love."

Agape love is the highest form of love. This is my favorite part of the definition to "demonstrate lavish goodness towards another person based on what is in their best interest." *Eros* (sensual love) is a valuable expression of love within the context of marriage. Girls often mistake sensual love for *agape* love. *Eros* love can trick them into thinking they are in a selfless, love relationship. They may experience physical, sensual, sexual feelings. None of that is "bad," but who wants *eros* without *agape* love? Outside of marriage, *eros* can turn in to lust. It is important for you in dating to be able to differentiate between *agape* love, and *eros* love.

*Eros* alone isn't good enough for one of my young friends anymore. She emailed me and said; "'Love' as I experienced, was the best feeling for me. I felt invincible. Looking back I would not really say that was love. Love now means to me being able to deny yourself, and most of all delay gratification by watching out for the other person…"

**Q** Is there such thing as a soulmate?

**A** My twenty-year-old friend, Abby, just asked me this question about soulmates last night. The concept of a soulmate is not something I have ever found in Scripture. My personal answer is no; there is not just one person out there for you. I believe we can love more than one person. God is *love* (1 John 4:8). He dwells in all believers. We have a well that never runs dry (John 4:10-13).

**Q** How do I know if he is "the one"?

**A** Three verses have profoundly influenced my decision making in most areas of my life. Consider how you could apply them to your life and to decisions about relationships.

**1. Colossians 3:15:** "And let the peace (soul harmony which comes) from Christ rule (act as umpire continually) in your hearts [deciding and settling with finality all questions that arise in your minds, in that peaceful state] . . ." (AMP).

Let me paraphrase this part of the verse for us: Let the peace of Christ decide with finality all of our questions. Notice the word *umpire* in the verse. I love that image. Peace gets to say "You're in!" or "You're out!" If I'm in a situation or relationship and I don't have peace, the Spirit will direct me with peace or a lack of it. Keep in mind, it is important to identify whether you are dealing with fear or a lack of peace about a dating relationship. They often look the same but are not. Let peace be your umpire.

**2. Philippians 2:13:** "[Not in your own strength] for it is God Who is all the while effectually at work in you [energizing and creating in you the power and desire], both to will and to work for His good pleasure and satisfaction and delight" (AMP).

I love this particular verse from Philippians so much, and it is the second verse I tend to go to when making a decision about something important in my life. Without judgment, I like to pay attention to the motivations and desires in my own heart. It's such a relational thing with God. Jeremiah was a Jewish Old Testament prophet who wrote under the Law of Moses. He says that the heart is "wicked." (Jeremiah 17:9, NKJV) Under the New Covenant we are given a new heart and a new mind, not a "wicked" one. Paying attention to our heart's desire is an opportunity to trust God. It requires faith. For instance, I have never wanted to write a book. All of a sudden, at 48 years old, I began to feel motivated and desired to write *unashamed.* So here I am writing, where this verse has led me. So look at the desires in your heart while you are dating someone. Does the relationship feel like the "unforced rhythms" of God's grace or does it feel like a lot of work (Matthew 11:28-30, The Message)? If it is of God that you are to be with this particular boy, the guy will experience and believe that too.

**3. Proverbs 11:14:** "Without good direction, people lose their way; the more wise counsel you follow, the better your chances" (The Message).

Anyone who knows me well knows I love to apply this verse. That is why I have brought together so many voices in this book. I think it is very important to give people you trust permission to offer you counsel. This includes their thoughts on any guy you date. Therefore, ask for counsel from some wise people in your life about the guy you are interested in.

**Q** **Is there a time that is too soon for someone to tell me that they love me or the other way around?**

**A** Hmm… If a guy says he loves you, I wonder which type of love he is referring to? Is it *phileo* (sisterly) love? Or *agape* (best interest) love? Perhaps *eros* (sensual) love? Identify what you are observing in his character, not just butterflies and feelings. Time and wisdom are crucial. I would recommend you lean on the side of caution in the beginning and let the relationship ride out a little bit before engaging in romantic love-talk.

**Q** **How young is too young to get married?**

**A** I was afraid a girl might ask this question. This is a subject that brings up all kinds of emotions in parents. I have one dear friend who got married at the age of eighteen. She is very opposed to young marriages. If you knew her story, you would understand her wisdom and caution on the subject. Others have gotten married very young and have awesome marriages. I'm an unconventional girl. If all parties were extremely healthy and mature, I would have been open to either of my kids getting married as early as nineteen.

Sometimes we treat young adults like kids for too long. They find themselves desiring *agape* and *eros* love for years. Plus super long engagements can be very challenging in the sexual temptation department. On another note, I'm also good with my kids finding their spouse much later in life, if that is what God has in store for them. As the Lord leads, I desire whatever is best for each person in each unique situation.

**Q** **When I am serious about a guy, are there certain questions or topics we should discuss before making a commitment?**

**A** We have already established in chapter three that it is not wise for a Christian to marry an unbeliever (2 Corinthians 6:14-15). Make sure you have a clear understanding of what the guy believes.

Other suggested topics for discussion include:
- faith
- praying together
- family history
- dreams and bucket lists
- shared interests
- hobbies and free-time
- career goals and expectations
- places you would like to live
- dream vacations (including with whom)
- how you like to experience church
- secrets
- conflict and fighting
- beliefs about counseling

- spending values and habits (including beliefs and desires in giving)
- current debt
- savings
- paying bills
- joint or separate accounts
- credit cards and loans
- loaning money to friends and family
- when you like to go to bed and when you like to wake up
- romance
- date nights
- TV in bedroom or not
- sex
- cleaning
- laundry
- which way toilet paper rolls should hang
- how many times you should use a towel
- yard work
- home improvement (to hire or not?)
- grocery shopping
- cooking
- pets
- how many children and when to begin trying
- childcare and parenting roles
- disciplining children
- private school, home-school, public school
- in-laws
- holidays

## A Word about Engagement

Don't enter into marriage lightly. If you get engaged, and start having a deep lack of peace about getting married: *Please, call it off!* Delay...even if you have already spent lots of money...even if you have gifts you will have to return...even if people will be frustrated with you. The stakes for you and your future children are in the making. You are not married until you're married. Yes, you're allowed to change your mind... even if you are engaged...even if the wedding is tomorrow.

**Q** What makes a good healthy marriage?

**A** Most people who get married want a good, loving, and healthy marriage.

Proverbs 13:12 says, "When the desire is fulfilled, it is a tree of life" (AMP).

It is important to note, that when you get married you are creating a "new" family. Jesus talks about this in Matthew 19:5: "And he said, 'This explains why a man leaves his father and mother and is joined to his wife, and the two are united into one" (NLT).

What does that mean for your parents? It means that you can still deeply love and honor your parents, but honor does not equal obedience. You and your new husband get to seek God for yourselves and agree on what works you for the two of you. Parents can be super-smart sometimes and they love you, so it can be great to seek their prayers and advice. However, you are never under an obligation to take it.

I just love that God chose the image of marriage to depict the relationship that all believers have with Christ. We are the bride. Christ is the groom. In Christ, we are given oneness with God as a gift (1 Corinthians 6:17). And yet, for marriage, "The two shall become one" (Matthew 19:5, NKJV). It does not say that the moment you get married that you *are* one. Notice the word "become". Becoming, is a sometimes painful, wonderful, messy process (Ephesians 5:25-31).

Some say marriage takes hard work. I personally wouldn't describe it that way. The great catalyst that made our marriage grow together over the years has been the Lord's work in each of us, individually (Philippians 1:6; 1 Thessalonians 5:24). In turn, this made us more delightful to each other.

I want to paint a simple picture of what is "good" to me. I was playing "The Well," a Casting Crowns song, the other day. I found myself spontaneously dancing around our kitchen. My husband was sitting there acting like that was completely normal. I am free to be me around him. *Unashamed.*

Bruce and I have a website for couples, called outsidethenest.net. It is a place where you will find inspiration and practical ideas on love and romance.

Here is a list we made from a recent blog we wrote. We are following up with a separate blog on each of these essentials.

**10 Essentials for a Fun, Healthy, and Lasting Marriage**

1. acceptance
2. communications
3. commitment
4. counsel
5. forgiveness
6. love
7. play
8. respect
9. sex
10. teamwork

Also, here is a great series on marriage by Pastor Pete Briscoe http://benttree.org/marriage/glue/

Bruce and I highly recommend it!

We also highly recommend reading the book, *The 5 Love Languages* by Gary Chapman.

Consider taking a few personality tests to learn more about each other. One we like is *StrengthsFinder* by Tom Rath.

**Q** I was taught growing up that sex was bad. How do I retrain my thinking before my wedding day, when all of a sudden I'm supposed to love it?

**A** Brilliant question. If you would indulge me for a moment: Let's play a little game.

- Is money bad? (The answer is no.)
- Can money be used for good? (Think of two good things.)
- Can money be used for bad? (Think of two icky things.)

- Does God think you are fearfully and wonderfully made? (Yes or no?)
- Whose idea was sex?
- Can sex be used in a super-sad way?
- Did God make sex to feel good?
- Can sex be beautiful to God?

If money isn't good or bad, then it's just a matter of how you use it. Think of sex the same way. It is not good or bad in itself. It's how you use it. Sex is like glue for a marriage. Sex is communication. Sex can be a fantastic expression of love. Sex can be satisfying and a blast. Sex can even be an expression of worship to God. Sex also makes really cute, precious babies.

**Q** **What do men in healthy marriages say about their wives?**

**A** Here is a response I got from my dear friend and neighbor John.

John: *"One of the things that makes Linda so amazing is that I truly don't know her, yet I'm captivated by knowing her. She smiles often and laughs frequently. It is a pleasure to search and discover the depths of my wife."*

Here is an excerpt from an email by a pastor friend of mine.

Jon: *"I tell young people often that God has one person for you, if you choose to marry, and that one person is the person you say "I do" to. Hard times? Sure. Difficulties? Absolutely. That is life. Certain words have to be removed from your vocabulary--words like "divorce" and "mine." And certain phrases have to be added, such as "Forgive me," "You are right," and "I'm wrong."*

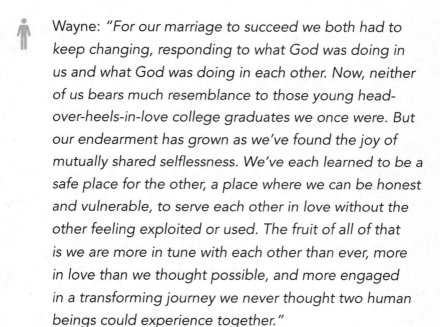

Wayne: *"For our marriage to succeed we both had to keep changing, responding to what God was doing in us and what God was doing in each other. Now, neither of us bears much resemblance to those young head-over-heels-in-love college graduates we once were. But our endearment has grown as we've found the joy of mutually shared selflessness. We've each learned to be a safe place for the other, a place where we can be honest and vulnerable, to serve each other in love without the other feeling exploited or used. The fruit of all of that is we are more in tune with each other than ever, more in love than we thought possible, and more engaged in a transforming journey we never thought two human beings could experience together."*

Bruce: *"It took a little time for me to realize marriage works best as a sphere. The circle works like this: she puts my needs before hers, I put her needs before before mine, and the love goes around and around."*

Doug: *"Her ability to love me, flawed and unlovable at times, was a mirror of how our heavenly Father loves us. That was a spark, an urging that led to a question one winter day in Paris: "Will you marry me?" To me, marriage has to be a commitment to achieve understanding no matter how difficult and no matter if compromise is required. That means the dialogue ranges from deep introspective questions and discussion to passionate argument. Healthy communication means a keen sense of knowing each other and each other's needs."*

**Q** What does healthy sexuality feel/look like?

**A** This topic would be best on the porch, age appropriate, with a great glass of wine or tall glass of lemonade with an engaged or married girl. But, since this book is primarily for single girls preparing for marriage, I will just mention a few things.

Communication about sex to your man needs to be tender, graceful, and honest. Be respectful and prayerful with your timing. I would never pretend sexually with my husband. Dishonesty never promotes marital intimacy. I Corinthians 7:4 says, "For the wife does not have [exclusive] authority and control over her own body, but the husband [has his rights]; likewise also the husband does not have [exclusive] authority and control over his body, but the wife [has her rights]" (AMP).

> *The goals:*
> *Have fun;*
> *be delightful;*
> *be playful;*
> *enjoy; love; be free,*
> *naked, and* **unashamed.**

II Corinthians 3:17 says: "For the Lord is the Spirit, and wherever the Spirit of the Lord is, there is freedom" (NLT).

God is intimately involved in your marital sex life. I have met several married Christian women who look at me like I'm an alien when I have shared that Bruce and I sometimes listen to praise music during sex or pray spontaneously as part of our sexual intimacy. God never leaves you. God celebrates when His married children enjoy each other.

One sensitive and important note: If you have sexual abuse in your background, please get some loving, grace-filled counseling before you enter into marriage. God can mend your soul. Allow God to heal you.

## Q What if my parents are divorced?

A First, I would imagine that their divorce was painful for you. I'm sorry for that. My thoughts? Forgive your parents, if necessary. Use the wisdom of what you learned for good. But honestly, you have nothing to fear. Get to know Christ, who dwells in all believers. He is the perfect husband. He will never divorce you. Bring that knowledge of His *love* into your marriage. As far as you are concerned, you are free to be healthy and committed to your future husband. You are creating a new family with your future spouse. 🍃

# unashamed

# chapter six

# God and the New Covenant

This is the last mile of our journey together in this book. I hope with all my heart, that you will stay with me through this final chapter. I promise it will be worth it.

Many years ago, I remember playing laser tag for the first time with another mom and our young kids. We went into the game without a strategy. The bell sounded and the festivities began. Everyone immediately filled their guns with bullets from our team's station. As they soon disappeared into the sea of neon and black, I noticed that no one was guarding our base, so I found myself spontaneously positioned to protect our turf. While I was there, I always made sure to keep my gun full, even if it was less than half empty. I never ran out of ammunition. I was in a wonderful position to protect base and help brave wounded, bullet-depleted teammates make it back to our resource. Once they were re-armed, off they went into the madness to make those risky and all-important shots for the team. And there I was, at base, almost the entire game.

Afterward, I wondered, what does the way I played the game say about me? I have often thought about that moment throughout the years. Here is what I have come to discover: the Gospel is home base for me. I have placed all my hope in Jesus. For me, as a former atheist, I just can't get over this salvation and life I have in Christ. Although I have been a Christian since 1996, since 2009 I have been steadily meditating on the love, grace, and the finished work of Jesus. This is the New Covenant and I want to write a whole chapter on it. I pray God can allow me to remind my brothers and sisters of the completed work of Jesus in the midst of the battles of life. Let's fill up and rediscover together what God has to say about His Son and what that means for you.

The first Bible verse I ever learned was: "In the multitude of counselors there is safety." (Proverbs 11:14, NKJV).

As I share my understanding of the New Covenant, I will apply this verse by providing a tapestry of wisdom from several of my favorite Bible teachers. Let me tell you why. Remember Lazarus? He was Jesus' dear friend who had died and was sealed in a tomb for four days. When he died, his family and friends dressed him, as was customary, in white linen cloths wrapping and binding his body. These were called grave clothes. When Jesus brought Lazarus to life, he was alive! But he still had these clothes binding him. I find it fascinating that Jesus Himself didn't take off the grave clothes. Jesus said to His family and friends, "Unbind him, and let him go" (John 11:44, NASB).

As believers we are like Lazarus, alive at the core. God often uses words of truth from other believers to unravel us from the grave-clothes of beliefs that bind us. New Covenant teaching undressed me of the shame I had carried around for so long. Therefore, in this chapter there will be many wise thinkers I have brought along for this discussion. Anyway, can I really do a better job than the Apostles Paul, Peter, John, or the writer of Hebrews?

## Q How does a person become a Christian?

**A** I just had a sweet friend in my living room this week who was wrestling with feeling unworthy of the love of God. Her struggle to believe she had value from God's perspective was intense. She needed to know that God proved how much He treasures us by sending His son, Jesus, to die for each one of us.

God values nothing more than His son, therefore, you must be worth a high price. That action displayed God's immense love and value for you personally. Yes, God loves and treasures you. Can you accept and agree with that?

I never want to reduce my life in Christ to a list or a formula. When I said, "yes" to Jesus, my life began to change forever. A *relationship* began. The word *gospel* means "good news." Good news is meant to be shared. I want to describe for you how I came into a relationship with Christ:

- I realized that I had sin in my life and wanted intimacy with God (Romans 3:23; 5:13-21).
- I came to believe that Jesus Christ was a real person and had lived a sinless life (2 Corinthians 5:21; Hebrews 4:15).

- By the encouragement of God's Spirit, I turned my heart toward Christ and agreed that He loved me and had really died on the cross for all my sins--past, present, and future (1 John 2:2; Hebrews 7:27).
- I received Jesus Christ and my old life was exchanged for His (Romans 6:5-11; Galatians 2:20).
- My eternity is secure in Christ (John 3:36).

Sometimes I wish I could see God and give Him a big hug.

Hebrews 11:1 says, "Now faith is the assurance (the confirmation, the title deed) of the things [we] hope for, being the proof of things [we] do not see . . ." (AMP). If you want to experience Christ, turn my list above into a prayer to God. Believe like a child--and be saved.

**Q** As a Christian, I know I am forgiven, but why do I still feel bad about myself sometimes?

**A** There were times in my earlier days of Christianity when I had this lingering sense of fear that I was not quite in God's good graces. It was like having a low-grade fever or melancholy spiritual hangover. I understand that you might feel "bad" about yourself from time to time. I believe the problem stems from basing our beliefs about our state of righteousness on our most recent behavior or perhaps our feelings. What we need to do is base our righteousness on what Christ has given believers permanently as a gift. Many Christians I have known believe their sins are forgiven and they will become righteous--one day, when they finally reach heaven. By believing we are still a little dirty, we assume we still need some level of self clean up. This all seems like the "normal Christian life." We are seduced into believing that God's presence and blessings are conditional. In our attempt to reach God, we make lists, read our Bibles, go to church, do some good deeds, and try to sin less. We often judge our worthiness and closeness to God by comparing the times we felt most holy and close to Him, to whatever behavioral and emotional state we currently find ourselves in. We are also tempted to evaluate ourselves in light of our perceptions of other believers. If they sin less than we do or have a job in a church building, surely, they must be on a higher spiritual level with God. We think we suck. Or, we look at our lives in comparison to people who are involved in lifestyles of intense sin. We conclude, perhaps, that we are doing pretty well compared to those guys. Either way, we are judging ourselves and others. Such comparisons only produce pride or shame. In the end we lose (1 Corinthians 4:4). I thought the Gospel was good news? This kind of thinking appears to be humble, but in reality it is "bad news." Ironically, this pathetic clean-thyself-up gospel makes a believer super *self* focused as opposed to "thank you, Jesus" focused.

The question was: "As a Christian, I know I am forgiven, but why do I still feel bad about myself sometimes?" I am severely dyslexic. I still couldn't read when I was in the third grade. Later, I became an actress. Then I met Jesus and discovered the Bible. Shakespeare sincerely didn't do it for me anymore. I had been looking for truth my whole life and had finally found it. God gave me a supernatural hunger and non-dyslexic ability to meditate and know Scripture. I pondered and memorized large portions of the Bible and hid much of the Word in my heart. As I applied Scripture, I experienced so many cool shifts in my life. Some of it was incredibly sweet, fulfilling, and life-giving. I encountered some healing from past wounds and much needed wisdom as I parented. I am grateful for that. But the deeper I went, the more I began to misunderstand passages that were not really written to me. You see, I used to read all the Bible with the same lens, as if somehow, all of it applied directly or indirectly to me. As you can imagine, I was inconsistent. But I tried. It didn't matter if a passage was in the Old Testament or the New Testament. I thought I should, at some level, obey it all. It was the Bible after all. God never changes. In my quest to "go big for God," it was a mixed bag; I had Spirit-filled moments of intimacy, revelation, and deep fellowship with God. Yet, I would break one "rule," make one "mistake," or sin, and that would catapult me into devastating deep disappointment or despair over my imperfection. My grace friends and I like to call that a "schizophrenic gospel." Some call that legalism. I was like the foolish Galatians who had come to Christ by faith, but believed I needed to do works of righteousness to justify myself for daily living.

Galatians 3:2-3 says, "Did you receive the Holy Spirit by obeying the law of Moses? Of course not! You received the Spirit because you believed the message you heard about Christ. How foolish can you be? After starting your new lives in the Spirit, why are you now trying to become perfect by your own human effort?" (NLT).

Pastor Paul White says, "If we don't know we are righteous, we will think we will become righteous by what we do...Our preoccupation is mostly with sin. We have actually defined spiritual growth in the church as the ability to avoid sin. The better you are at avoiding sin, the more mature we say you are in Christ...Absolutely wrong, our preoccupation with sin has kept us from being occupied with our righteousness."[12]

Over time, I became more religious. I am using the word *religious* here in a burdensome way. You might say I was striving for self-righteousness, as opposed to trusting in Christ's righteousness. In rule-focused religion, people often trade enjoying their relationship with God for works (Galatians 5:1-13). This mindset increasingly stole a level of assurance and joy that I had experienced when I first came into Christ.

John 10:10 says, ". . . I came that they may have and enjoy life, and have it in abundance (to the full, till it overflows)" (AMP). I wish I had understood the New Covenant all those years. Then I would have believed what Christ accomplished on the cross makes me forever close to Him and completely, permanently clean.

Never accept anything less than the complete perfection of Christ.

The Mosaic Law might be what you're struggling with. The Jewish law is not for me and was never instituted to produce righteousness or life. Its function relied ultimately on its ability to point people to Christ.

Galatians 3:24 says, "So that the Law served [to us Jews] as our trainer [our guardian, our guide to Christ, to lead us] until Christ [came], that we might be justified (declared righteous, put in right standing with God) by and through faith" (AMP).

---

12 www.paulwhiteministries.com

I am *not* throwing out the Old Testament or the law. The Mosaic Covenant is a beautiful shadow intended to direct us into the arms of our Savior. Although I respect the Jewish law, it does not *apply* to me as a Christian. Jesus fulfilled it (Romans 10:4).

Let's look at Romans 7:6: "But now we are discharged from the Law and have terminated all intercourse with it, having died to what once restrained and held us captive. So now we serve not under [obedience to] the old code of written regulations, but [under obedience to the promptings] of the Spirit in newness [of life]" (AMP).

Pay close attention to this next verse. Look for a word that is repeated twice. Hebrews 8:13: "When God speaks of a new [covenant or agreement], He makes the first one obsolete (out of use). And what is obsolete (out of use and annulled because of age) is ripe for disappearance and to be dispensed with altogether" (AMP).

*Obsolete.* Did you notice that word used twice in the scripture above? I remember when I first got a hold of that word. Webster's Dictionary says it means: "no longer used because something newer exists: replaced by something newer".[13] I used to believe I needed to submit, fulfill, and obey rules I perceived from Old Covenant passages. Don't get me wrong; there was nothing evil about my intentions. There were no bad motives when I searched my church world for modern day pseudo-laws (quiet time, church attendance, avoiding bad words, etc.) I just wanted to do Christianity "right." And there certainly was no lack of teachers out there telling me all the things I needed to do to please God. I was sincere and

---

13 Merriam Webster, Merriamwebster.com.

full of love in my attempts to improve myself and others. I was putting myself under *laws* and had no understanding of how Jesus had made the Old Covenant obsolete by fulfilling it (Luke 22:20, Hebrews 8:13).

I was sincere when it came to interpreting Scripture; however, in some instances I was sincerely wrong. Here is the worst part: I began to put a religious burden and expectation on my lighthearted Christian husband. He began to believe he was unworthy of being my spiritual equal. The enemy took advantage of this opportunity (Ephesians 6:12). Bruce's doubts became so profound, that at one point, he considered leaving the marriage. Which was totally not cool, and definitely not God's heart. But, you see, my husband naturally has no tolerance for legalism. My confusion and misapplication of scripture almost contributed to the downfall of my marriage (Galatians 5:9). I am not exaggerating

The schizophrenic gospel almost cost me the most precious person in my life. It was something I struggled with for years, until my spiritual mentor, John Sheasby, taught me I was "mixing covenants" (Galatians 3:1-14).

People like me ultimately want truth at all costs. Even if it means they need to reconsider their view on something. N. T. Wright writes, "True wisdom is both bold and humble. It is never afraid to say what it thinks it has seen, but will always covet other angles of vision."[14]

---

14 N.T. Wright, *Surprised by Scripture.*

**Q** Explain what you mean by the word *covenants*?

**A** Remember Scripture is written on our behalf, but not all of it was written directly *to* us. In submitting to a passage, it is crucial to correctly divide the word of truth (2 Timothy 2:15). We need to know the *context* of a passage, who is being addressed and which covenant these individuals are under.

A covenant is a binding promise between two or more parties. For our purposes, we will talk about three covenants found in the Bible.

**1. The Abrahamic Covenant**
Remember Abraham? He was actually asleep when God created this covenant. He had a covenant of faith, not works. Abraham committed adultery and lied. God calls Abraham His friend and righteous. The Lord promises to greatly and miraculously bless him, not counting his sins against him (James 2:23). I'll elaborate more on Abraham's covenant later in this chapter.

**2. The Mosaic Covenant**
This covenant with Israel was ushered in by Moses on tablets of stone, the Ten Commandments. In addition to that, consider more than 600 commands—roughly 300 positive and 300 negative. Yikes! The law demanded that Jewish people perform rituals and sacrifices. Those sacrifices were an annual reminder of sins. Under these conditions, God blesses obedience and curses disobedience. Unlike Abraham's covenant, the Mosaic covenant promises are conditional.

Hebrews 7:19 says, "...the law made nothing perfect" (NKJV).

## 3. The New Covenant

Hebrews 8:7 says: "For if there had been nothing wrong with that first covenant, no place would have been sought for another" (NLT). Clarification: when the Book of Hebrews refers to the first covenant here, it is referring to the Law of Moses.

The prophet, Jeremiah, predicted that there would be a time when God would make a New Covenant (Jeremiah 31:31-33) This New Covenant would someday be written in believers' hearts.

Hebrews 8:10-12, NKJV, says:

*For this is the covenant that I will make with the house of Israel after those days, says the Lord: I will put My laws in their mind and write them on their hearts; and I will be their God, and they shall be My people. None of them shall teach his neighbor, and none his brother, saying, "Know the Lord" for all shall know Me, from the least of them to the greatest of them. For I will be merciful to their unrighteousness, and their sins and their lawless deeds I will remember no more.*

Let's be careful when we read the word *law* here. I have seen many believers and teachers, including myself, assume the word *law* means the same thing in every case in the Bible. *Law* is not a one-word-fits-all term. Many might say, "The Lord writes the law of Moses on your heart in the New Covenant." He does not. Each Covenant has its own terms of agreement. The Mosaic Covenant has its own separate terms. The Mosaic Law under the Old Covenant required Jewish women on their period to move into a separate tent. It also required women to keep their hair kempt or "you will die" (Leviticus 10:6). It forbade the eating of pork or shell fish and banned touching an unclean animal. (Leviticus 5:2). Jews were not allowed to mix fabrics in clothing (Leviticus 19:19). The Jewish law outlawed the crossbreeding of animals (Leviticus 19:19). The Mosaic Law even barred tattoos (Leviticus 19:28). Oops! Bruce is in trouble!! He has a really cool tattoo on his ankle. Since I mentioned it, we have asked our kids to wait on that issue until they are off the payroll. A tattoo is a pretty long-term commitment. I digress. Anyway…

Well actually, one more rabbit trail. I was explaining that I see a distinction between the two biblical Covenants, the Old and New, to my darling, inquisitive friend Kerrie, just last night. I said, "Let's take a look at both of our marriages. Your marriage and my marriage are two separate covenants. There are certain benefits exclusive to my covenant with my husband. You don't get the benefits of being married to Bruce. My man does not provide for you or sleep with you, and he has made no promise to you. Nor has your husband to me. Legally, you do not have any rights in my covenant, neither do I have any rights to yours." My hope with that analogy was to begin to demonstrate a distinction between the Old Covenant and the New Covenant. Just like the separate marriage promises, we have no obligations under the first covenant, and furthermore have all the benefits and rights that belong to those within this New Covenant.

Hebrews 8:6 says: "But now Jesus, our High Priest, has been given a ministry that is far superior to the old priesthood, for he is the one who mediates for us a far better covenant with God, based on better promises" (NLT). The author of Hebrews here is describing better terms under a better covenant than the Law of Moses. Check out what Pastor Paul

White says about the good news of this New Covenant, as written in Hebrews: "Read it slowly and soak it in believer: no more offering for sin (Hebrews 10:18). No more lambs need be killed; no more priests need to work the altars. Jesus has paid our sin debt and now no more blood must be shed... Rest against the backbone of the New Covenant; the fact that God chooses to remember your sins no more. Hallelujah!"[15]

Hebrews 7:27 says: "Unlike those other high priests, he does not need to offer sacrifices every day. They did this for their own sins first and then for the sins of the people. But Jesus did this once for all when he offered himself as the sacrifice for the people's sins" (NLT).

Under the New Covenant, Christ dwells in believers, so He is *always* close. Also, in this New Covenant, believers are declared permanently clean because of Christ's blood. We are not just covered in righteousness; we are made new. Like I said, I can't say it better than the writer of Hebrews. I am a daughter of the New Covenant.

## Q When did the New Covenant begin?

## A Great question!

Hebrews 9:16 says, "For where a covenant is, there must of necessity be the death of the one who made it" (NASB).

Notice the word *death* in the sentence above. You see, the New Covenant does not really begin on that first New Testament page of your Bible. It does not begin on Jesus'

---

15 www.paulwhiteministries.wordpress.com

birthday. The New Covenant is brought about by the death and resurrection of Jesus.

Pay special attention to what Jesus did and says at the Last Supper: "He took some bread and gave thanks to God for it. Then he broke it in pieces and gave it to the disciples, saying, "This is my body, which is given for you. Do this to remember me." After supper he took another cup of wine and said, "This cup is the new covenant between God and his people—an agreement confirmed with my blood, which is poured out as a sacrifice for you." (Luke 22:19-20, NLT).

It matters when the New Covenant began. With a New Covenant comes a new set of promises. In this case, better promises. Hebrews 8:6 says, ". . . He is also Mediator of a better covenant, which was established on better promises" (NKJV).

There are many things Jesus says to His Jewish audience before He dies. Remember, they were under the Mosaic Law with its promises of blessings and curses based on obedience. Christ had not died yet in passages like the Sermon on the Mount (Matthew 5-7). Under a New Covenant, if we assume those teachings are for Christians to apply, we will end up in bondage. I must consider the audience He is speaking to and correctly divide between covenants. For instance, before the cross, Jesus says: "If you forgive those who sin against you, your heavenly Father will forgive you. But if you refuse to forgive others, your Father will not forgive your sins" (Matthew 6:14, NLT).

Or how about the prayer Jesus taught to the Jews before He went to the cross: "and forgive us our sins, as we have forgiven those who sin against us" (Matthew 6:12, NLT).

That's pretty scary. Under that teaching to the Jews, before the cross, my forgiveness is dependent on me, not on Christ. Yikes! What if I forget one? That is not good news. Wait a minute, what ever happened to Hebrews 8:12? "For I will be merciful and gracious toward their sins and I will remember their deeds of unrighteousness no more" (AMP).

Now we are back to a schizophrenic gospel. Are we forgiven or not? Here is the key: Ask yourself *how* and *when* we are forgiven?

Romans 6:10 says, "For the death that He died, He died to sin once for all . . . " (NASB) and Colossians 2:13 says, ". . . he forgave all our sins" (NLT).

*How* did we get forgiven? By the blood of Christ. *When* does He remember no more? Each time we ask? No! It was *once and for all. It is finished* (John 19:30). No morsel of forgiveness is withheld from Christians. You do not have to do anything to be more forgiven.

Let's say I have a conversation with a friend. And at some point in the discussion, I find myself talking about another believer who did something I didn't like. And let's assume I am not seeking counsel from this friend, but I am acting ugly, and I find myself gossiping. Assume I have no real peace about my diarrhea of the mouth. I know that is gross, but sin isn't pretty. Afterwards, I can sense that I have grieved the Holy Spirit by gossiping in that moment (Ephesians 4:20). When I am driving home in my car and reflecting on the conversation, I might say something like this to the Lord:

> "Lord, I just gossiped about one of your kids. Why did I do that? I could sense a lack of peace about what I was saying, but I just kept on going. I know I have self-

*control, but I didn't use it. I'm really sorry Lord. I know I
am a forgiven person and what I did does not make me
bad. You are fine with me. You love me. I am still just
as clean now as I was the moment you saved me. Lord,
would you help me to not do that again?"*

Confession is agreeing with God. Here, I am simply
concurring with God that sin is stupid and *not* who I am in
Christ. I am coming into agreement with the truth. Agreeing
with God is renewing your mind in what is true. I do not
believe I receive an ounce of new righteousness or forgiveness
by agreeing with God about the fact that sin makes me sad
and is not what I am made for. But I do agree and celebrate
His total and "once for all" forgiveness for me that occurred
long ago. And if I don't confess, I am still forgiven. I am still
clean. He is still as close as ever. God is still dwelling in me.

I am about to share more Scripture and longer quotes.
I want to prove to you that you really can rest in the finished
work of Jesus. I don't want you to believe for one more second
that God is far from you. I long for you to agree with God that
He has made you permanently clean.

## Q Why does Abraham matter?

**A** Now, let's go back to Abraham and his covenant. You
know, he was around before the old Mosaic Covenant.
His was a covenant of unconditional promises.

Galatians 3:7-14, NLT says:

*The real children of Abraham, then, are those who
put their faith in God. What's more, the Scriptures looked
forward to this time when God would declare the Gentiles*

*to be righteous because of their faith. God proclaimed this good news to Abraham long ago when he said, "All nations will be blessed through you." So all who put their faith in Christ share the same blessing Abraham received because of his faith. But those who depend on the law to make them right with God are under his curse, for the Scriptures say, "Cursed is everyone who does not observe and obey all the commands that are written in God's Book of the Law." So it is clear that no one can be made right with God by trying to keep the law. For the Scriptures say, "It is through faith that a righteous person has life." This way of faith is very different from the way of law, which says, "It is through obeying the law that a person has life." But Christ has rescued us from the curse pronounced by the law. When he was hung on the cross, he took upon himself the curse for our wrongdoing. For it is written in the Scriptures, "Cursed is everyone who is hung on a tree." Through Christ Jesus, God has blessed the Gentiles with the same blessing he promised to Abraham, so that we who are believers might receive the promised Holy Spirit through faith.*

Notice again, that in the Abrahamic Covenant, the blessings of God come by faith, not works. And notice that one of the blessings is the Holy Spirit. That is the key to the next question.

**Q** What do we do about sin in light of the New Covenant?

**A** "The obstacle to experiencing victory over temptation is the way in which we've gone about the battle. When we arm ourselves with the law, we set ourselves up for failure every time. We may call it self-discipline or accountability – or plug in some other inventive term. But when it's anything but dependency on Christ within us, it'll inevitably put the wheels of human effort in motion."[16]

Romans 8:1-2 says, "So now there is no condemnation for those who belong to Christ Jesus. And because you belong to him, the power of the life-giving Spirit has freed you from the power of sin that leads to death" (NLT). As a Christian, I will never believe that you or I are void of power over sin. That is such good news. The problem usually occurs when believers don't *believe* they possess power over sin. Power is not the problem. What you believe is the issue. Do you believe that the Spirit that raised Jesus from the dead has freed you from the power of sin? I do.

I want you to know what another one of my favorite Bible teachers, Frank Viola has to say about sin in light of the New Covenant: "Hebrews exhorts us to come boldly to the 'throne of grace' (4:16). Where God's people are concerned, Jesus Christ sits on a throne of grace, not a throne of judgment...When you feel condemned for something you've done wrong, you are essentially making yourself an idol. Why? Because you're setting your opinion over God's opinion."[17]

"Many Christians just do not grasp the Father's mercy and grace. We are unable to see ourselves as God sees us. We are so self-conscious; the recorded memories of the past and the misunderstanding of the gospel combine to blind our eyes to the truth....'Behold the Lamb,'... Not once did the priest

---

16  Andrew Farley, *The Naked Gospel*
17  Frank Viola, *Jesus Now*

examine the worshiper! Not once!... Where is your focus? The Lamb or yourself?"[18]

I love the point John makes here. I remember when I first grasped this concept. The Jews needed a blood sacrifice for sins. They didn't try to clean themselves up. They believed that God accepted an animal sacrifice for sins. It wasn't about their behavior. They were counting on the sacrifice. I find it interesting that we, as Christians tend to think it's up to us to satisfy God's righteousness. If we followed the sacrificial line of thinking we would realize that Christ, once for all, died as a sacrifice for our sins. We also would be able to rest.

People who don't really understand the New Covenant often misunderstand it as a license to sin. I have heard others criticize the message of grace in their ignorance. New Covenant is not pro-sin. The Spirit never leads a believer to sin.

Let's settle it now. If you're a Christian, you are a daughter of the New Covenant. God isn't mad at you. God is near. Your sins are forgiven.

## Q What about the Ten Commandments?

## A The Ten Commandments are under the Law of Moses, not under the New Covenant.

Acts 13:38-39 says, "Brothers, listen! We are here to proclaim that through this man Jesus there is forgiveness for your sins. Everyone who believes in him is declared right with God—something the law of Moses could never do" (NLT).

---

18 John Sheasby, *The Birthright*

All Scripture is God-breathed, yes (2 Timothy 3:16). But it can bring death to areas of your life if you mix covenants. Take a look at these comments from Andrew Farley: "How do we live upright lives if we don't use the Ten Commandments as our guide?…Principles, rules, standards – no matter how "Christian" we believe they are – are poor substitutes for a life animated by God himself."[19]

And from Andrew Farley's Facebook page on October 29, 2013:

> We can't divide God's law into categories and then pick the parts we want. If we want to be under the Law, then we are cursed for not keeping all of it. James and Paul do not speak merely of 10 things or of nine things as we choose to exclude the Sabbath. No, the apostles speak of 613 commands of the Law…It's a death trap. I'm not against the Law, and I don't disrespect the Law. I don't even teach that the Law is dead or abolished. But we Christians are dead to the Law. Big difference.

Hang in there, girls. Take a break if you need to. When you're ready, read the Scripture passages below. I wrote them on our chalkboard in our home more than five years ago…

II Corinthians 3:16-17: "Whenever, though, they turn to face God as Moses did, God removes the veil and there they are—face-to-face! They suddenly recognize that God is a living, personal presence, not a piece of chiseled stone. And when God is personally present, a living Spirit, that old, constricting legislation is recognized as obsolete. We're free of it!" (The Message). That is a beautiful verse. One more.

---

19 Andrew Farley, *The Naked Gospel.*

Galatians 2:16, (AMP):

*Yet we know that a man is justified or reckoned righteous and in right standing with God not by works of the Law, but [only] through faith and [absolute] reliance on and adherence to and trust in Jesus Christ (the Messiah, the Anointed One). [Therefore] even we [ourselves] have believed on Christ Jesus, in order to be justified by faith in Christ and not by works of the Law [for we cannot be justified by any observance of the ritual of the Law given by Moses], because by keeping legal rituals and by works no human being can ever be justified (declared righteous and put in right standing with God).*

The Ten Commandments are not your guide for righteousness. The Ten Commandments were written after Abraham and to Jews exclusively. The Law of Moses put the Jewish nation into a binding agreement with God. Back in the day, no Jew would ever look at a Gentile (a non-Jewish person) and expect him or her to submit to the laws of the Old Covenant. Why do we so often do that now? Guess what? Jesus fulfilled the Law of Moses (Matthew 5:17).

Romans 10:3 says: "For they don't understand God's way of making people right with himself. Refusing to accept God's way, they cling to their own way of getting right with God by trying to keep the law" (NLT).

Andrew Farley writes: "Once we are placed in Christ at salvation, we completely die to the law and resurrect in Christ, led by the Spirit, with no need for the law in our lives."[20]

Romans 10:4 says: "For Christ is the end of the law for righteousness to everyone who believes" (NKJV). Christians

---

20 Andrew Farley, *Relaxing with God*

are now under a very freeing and different *law* in the New Covenant. And it is not one of free-wheeling chaos where you hurt yourself and others. It is called "the law of the Spirit of life." As a believer, you have the Holy Spirit now as your guide. God has lavishly poured His love into your heart (Romans 5:5) and provided for you to love Him back, and love others well. He has great plans for you, child of God.

 **How do we live under the New Covenant?**

There are at least four ways: *believe, rest, enjoy,* and *walk in Spirit-led good works.*

### Believe

Believe that God loves you. Let's pause at the thought of that. I pray this truth might go beyond your human capacity for understanding. How about right now, take time to meditate on *God, Jesus* and the Holy *Spirit's* love for you being higher than you can conceptualize the galaxies above you. Take a moment to pause on that thought....Picture God's love for you being profoundly deep. Take your time . . . Next, know His love is endlessly wide for you; can you see it? . . . Finally, imagine His love like a path laid out before you; this path is outrageously long, like a road that never ends... (Ephesians 3:14-21)

Here is more "good news" to believe. Galatians 2:20 says: "My old self has been crucified with Christ. It is no longer I who live, but Christ lives in me. So I live in this earthly body by trusting in the Son of God, who loved me and gave himself for me" (NLT).

Colossians 3:3 says: "For [as far as this world is concerned] you have died, and your [new, real] life is hidden with Christ in God" (AMP).

Do you believe you can be *naked* and *unashamed* before the Lord? Naked in every sense, that you are free to be yourself and at ease with no shame.

Galatians 3:27 says: "For all of you who were baptized into Christ have clothed yourselves with Christ" (NASB). Ladies, a secret has been revealed: You are not even naked now after all. You are hidden and clothed in Christ, dressed in His righteousness alone. Our son, Josh, is a songwriter and he put this truth into a recent song:

*"Let me hide in your promise*
*That I am found in you*
*And just in case I've forgotten*
*That you're found in me too*
*'Cause there is just no space between*
*I'm your friend and you love me*
*So as I'm found in your promise*
*It gives me joy to sing*

*You're reaching out to me with arms stretched wide*
*I finally see the plan in your great design*
*That every little part of me, is drenched*
*in the water that says I'm free*
*Drowning as I feast, on the river that gives me peace*

*I can rest in the unchanging, inside a love that's so amazing*

*It is finished and you have saved me, a holy child is what*
*you've named me*
*You gave me peace like a river, you've shown*
*me wings that soar*
*You covered me with your mercy, now all my debt's paid for."*[21]

II Corinthians 5:17 says: "This means that anyone who belongs to Christ has become a new person. The old life is gone; a new life has begun!" (NLT). My daughter Caroline recently reminded me that, "Jesus didn't come to make bad people good. He came to make dead people alive."

Andrew Farley teaches: "The phrase 'die to self' is nowhere to be found in the Scripture. The closest thing we find is that "our old self was crucified" (Romans 6:6). It's happened. We are new creations."

"Interview with Pastor, Professor and Author of God without Religion: Andrew Farley."[22]

Here is a promise from Ephesians 1:13: "In Him, you also, after listening to the message of truth, the gospel of your salvation—having also believed, you were sealed in Him with the Holy Spirit of promise" (NASB).

I was at the gym early yesterday. There was an attractive man who kept trying to have a conversation with me. You see, I forgot to wear my wedding ring. That ring symbolizes that I am taken, that I belong to Bruce. If you are a Christian, you have a ring too. His name is the Holy Spirit and He has put a ring around you, a seal. The Spirit dwells in you. You are taken. Even better, you cannot take your ring off or forget to put it on.

---

21  Josh Levinson, *Peace Like a River.*
22  Mattlitton.com.

Acts 7:48 says: "However, the Most High does not dwell in houses and temples made with hands; as the prophet says" (AMP). You get to live freely by the Spirit that indwells you. Ezekiel 36:26 says: "And I will give you a new heart, and I will put a new spirit in you. I will take out your stony, stubborn heart and give you a tender, responsive heart" (NLT).

How do we make decisions by the Spirit? We pay attention to His peace and His promptings (Colossians 3:15). You are equipped (Philippians 2:13) Second Peter 1:3 says: "By his divine power, God has given us everything we need for living a godly life" (NLT).

Here are some fun, practical suggestions for the renewing of your mind in the truth of the New Covenant (Romans 12:2). Consider these, as God leads you.

Meditate on the goodness of God.

Study Galatians and Hebrews.

Listen to the song *The Well* by Casting Crowns.

Listen to the album *Welcome to the New* by Mercy Me.

Read *The Naked Gospel* and *Resting with God*, by Andrew Farley.

Read *The Birthright* by John Sheasby.

I dare you to watch www.youtube.com/watch?v=S0KRj3TH1oA (by John Lynch).

Listen to the podcasts of Andrew Farley, Paul White, Judah Smith (our son Josh's favorite).

Listen to John Sheasby's podcasts on the New Covenant at www.liberatedliving.com

Listen to the series on www.city.org, *"Jesus is Bringing Sexy Back"* by Judah Smith (incredible).

Most importantly, meditate on the love of God.

This is my prayer for you, from Ephesians 3:14 -18: "I fall to my knees and pray…Your roots will grow down into God's love and keep you strong. And may you have the power to understand, as all God's people should, how wide, how long, how high, and how deep his love is." (NLT).

## *Rest*

I so long for you to know you can trust in the finished work of Jesus and let your soul finally rest.

Acts 17:28 says: "For in Him we live and move and have our being…" (AMP). We are in Him; He is in us. I love how the writer of Hebrews says to be "diligent" to enter the Lord's rest (Hebrews 4:1-16).

John Sheasby writes: "The pattern of Jesus' life on earth gives insight into God's method of transformation. He knows that you, like Zacchaeus, will not be changed by performance, but by his presence. The power of his love, the joy of his presence, and the peace coming from his acceptance are far more capable of changing the human heart than rebuke, censure, condemnation, and rejection."[23]

The Lord will do the work of transforming our lives to reflect His goodness. First Thessalonians 5:24 says: "God will make this happen, for he who calls you is faithful (NLT).

Pastor Paul White writes: "The message of grace holds up nothing but Jesus and His finished work…The single most important thing that you will do from now until the day you die is to labor to stay in His rest."[24]

I have kept this quote from seminary Professor Howard Hendricks on my bulletin board for 12 years now. I am finally

---

23 John Sheasby, *The Birthright.*
24 Paul White, *Revelation to Transformation.*

beginning to understand it: "The Holy Spirit has developed in me an incurable confidence in His ability to transform people."[25]

 As I rest in God, I have learned to pray and worship Him without turning it into a work. I don't want to do anything under compulsion or because I think I have to, so, I pray as I feel led, not under pressure. When prayer becomes an obligation or a work instead of a conversation with my Abba/ Daddy I am missing the point (Romans 8:15). When people around me sing songs to God, I might join in, if I feel inspired. But often, you will find me quietly sitting before the Lord... because I want to worship Him in spirit and in *truth* (John 4:24). I never sing lyrics of songs that ask God to rain down His presence. I also tend to remain silent on choruses that tell God I am running after Him, because I spend my thoughts believing that *He is already present and that I am lacking nothing. I can't run after Him, because He would just travel with me, since He never leaves me.* This is New Covenant thinking. This thinking has set me free.

### Enjoy

Jesus came to bring you life. You are meant to richly enjoy life. This includes healthy relationships with your brothers in Christ and your future spouse. Jesus said in John 10:10: "I came that they may have and enjoy life, and have it in abundance (to the full, till it overflows)" (AMP).

 A few years ago I really started meditating on the concept of enjoying life. One of my favorite restaurants in New York City is called Serendipity3. On their website they joyfully

---

25 "The Life of Howard G. "Prof' Hendricks," www.dts.edu, DTS Magazine.

write, "ser.en.dip.i.ty (n) the art of making happy discoveries, or finding the unexpectedly pleasant, by chance or sagacity."[26]

Here are a few phrases I still keep on my bulletin board from that season of learning how to embrace life:

- "Because life is short make it lovely."
- "Live Well."
- "Every man dies, but not every man really lives."[27]

As my understanding of the New Covenant evolved, I finally started enjoying my life in Christ and allowed myself to really "live." The funny thing is, as I began to relax and have more fun and be a more joyful person, God surprised me. Some incredible moments involved the wonder of leading people to Christ, like a painter named Joe and a plumber named Thomas. I found myself doing things I would have previously judged as shallow or unspiritual. And yet, God placed me perfectly in a position to do good, exactly where He wanted me, as I relaxed and enjoyed life. This understanding also brought great delight to my marriage. My husband found this joyful, fun, peaceful, free person much more attractive.

Bruce isn't afraid to celebrate life and is really big on making bucket-lists, or some might say goal lists. But his dreams are not full of "shoulds," they are specific goals that would bring him great joy. In typical Bruce fashion, his bucket list is hilarious and fun. He has actually done many items on his agenda, such as throwing out the first pitch in a baseball stadium.

I stopped doing New Year's resolutions about ten years ago based on the reality that I ended up feeling *bad* about

---

26 www.serendipity3.com
27 Mel Gibson as William Wallace in the movie *Brave Heart.*

not measuring up to my own list. I have noticed, especially when it comes to concepts like losing weight, that I personally don't know anyone who has kept the weight off, long-term by following "rules." So, I wondered, is there a more gentle, positive, delightful, and more winsome approach to discovering and creating an enjoyable life?

Several years ago I was sitting on our porch with a friend of mine and two college students. I began to ask each of the women about their hopes and desires. Then I had an idea! So I ran inside and got some extra large note cards and pencils so we could play a game. Do you want to play?

If so, go grab a pencil, and some paper, a journal or some note cards.

Here's what I asked: "If you were free to dream without fear or judging your own desires as silly, shallow, unattainable, selfish--truly free to dream—what would make your heart happy, if it occurred in your life? Realistic or not, just dream."

Now write down the top ten things for this current season that would make you happy, in any order. So we all sat there with our big note cards and began to scribble down our secret longings. (This exercise can also be great in creating a "wish" list for character traits you want to look for in a guy or a job).

Then I asked them to circle their top three. So if you're playing along, will you circle your top three?

Next, I told them to, "Put a 1, 2, 3 next to their top three in order of strongest desire, with 1 being the top one." Again, stressing no judgment or *shoulds*, I discouraged thoughts like: "Well, I *should* want *this one* over *that one*." I encouraged them to simply allow what would make their *heart happy* lead the order. Then we began to go around and share each number one with each other. It was like we were giving the dreams a chance to breath and come out to play. It was fascinating. Some dreams were completely out of our control, like those concerning someone else's health. Or, unrealistic, like the secret that I have always wanted to be a tiny fairy. That's not going to happen. But, if applicable, we began to brainstorm about steps each person could possibly take on a journey towards their hopes and goals. Often ideas were said that were something the writer of the goal wouldn't have thought of on her own.

This spontaneous exercise has grown into several years of bucket-list parties. Something profound happens when we share our top things on our pieces of paper. You get a tiny glimpse into a person's heart, and you begin to care about what they care about. It's fun to celebrate when change occurs for a person in an area. We have seen some amazing results over the years. Sadly, I am not a fairy...yet.

### *Walk in Spirit-Led Good Works*

Ephesians 2:10 says: "For we are God's [own] handiwork (His workmanship), recreated in Christ Jesus, [born anew] that we may do those good works which God predestined (planned beforehand)" (AMP). My prayer is that you are believing, resting in, and enjoying God. From that position, there are some pretty cool people He wants you to enjoy, love, and perhaps serve. Opportunities will arise for you to use some of the difficulties of your life for good. You can be a great encouragement to others as the Lord leads you. II Corinthians 1:3-4 says: ". . . God is our merciful Father and the source of all comfort. He comforts us in all our troubles so that we can comfort others. When they are troubled, we will be able to give them the same comfort God has given us" (NLT).

There are certainly fulfilling, good things God will want to involve you in. But it is His job to reveal them to you. Philippians 2:13 says: "For it is God who works in you both to will and to do for His good pleasure" (NKJV).

Here is a verse I would like you to read with New Covenant glasses. With no condemnation or pressure. See if you can't discover a clue about knowing where God is at work in your life: "Let each one [give] as he has made up his own mind and purposed in his heart, not reluctantly or sorrowfully or under compulsion, for God loves…a cheerful (joyous . . .), giver" (2 Corinthians 9:7, AMP). This verse is not God telling you to *do* anything. It is *not* a verse written so you can judge your giving and say to yourself "I should be more cheerful; what is wrong with me?" It is a great verse to see where God is at work in your life. When it sounds fun and/or desirable to give your resources or time to someone or something, being cheerful is a great clue that God might be leading you. There will always be needs. You are not to fulfill them all just because they show up on your doorstep. Jesus did not go to every town. He just did what the Father instructed Him to do (John 5:19).

And don't forget Peace. Peace is a person. His name is Jesus. He is the Prince of Peace. And He dwells in you. What if someone asks you to do something or you see a need, but have an icky feeling about it? I say, don't do it. Wait. Remember, Colossians 3:15 says: "And let the peace (soul harmony which comes) from Christ rule (act as umpire continually) in your hearts [deciding and settling with finality all questions that arise in your minds, in that peaceful state] to which as [members of Christ's] one body you were also called [to live] . . ." (AMP). Remember this verse. Be still. Fear is not in charge. Wait for peace in your decisions. The Prince of Peace reigns. Let Him guide you. Believe Him. Rest in Him. Enjoy Him. Wait with Him. Then, move as the Spirit leads you.

the end

*Okay girls,*
*I'm feeling a little sad just now.*
*Because I am drawing near to the end of the page.*
*I didn't even know I was going to write a book until*
*my Pastor friend Alan Smith gently challenged me*
*to consider it.*
*So one day, I began to type--and I couldn't stop.*
*Who knew I had so much to share?*
*I suppose God did.*
*It must have been a good work He planned in*
*advance for me to walk in.*
*So here you have it; A collection of questions,*
*Scriptures, stories, quotes, ponderings, and words*
*of protective love.*
*I am a child of God, a wife, and a mother,*
*but in the end, I'm a girl just like you.*
*Thanks for hanging out with me for the journey*
*of this book.*
*I am unashamed;*
*I am profoundly moved;*
*I am deeply blessed.*
*I miss you already...*

♥

# unashamed

# afterword

Caroline Levinson

I want to tell you about my mom. She is passionate, authentic, wise, a deep lover, and a ray of sunshine in the darkest places.

As you read this book, did you sense that she loves you deeply? She actually does. My mom is full of grace and truth. She, more than anyone I know, longs for the truth to be known. John 8:32 says: "And you will know the truth, and the truth will set you free" (NLT). If anyone can be a testament to this passion of hers, it would be me. In high school, my friends and I would sometimes laugh uncontrollably as she acted out stories/parables to describe some sort of biblical truth. Now, when I bring college friends home with me to seek a weekend of rest, she invests hours of compassionate listening and counsel, as we process dreams and concerns about our futures. I often see her chatting with women of all ages, as she sits in an egg-shaped swinging chair on the family porch. Sometimes, she is hopping in the car to meet a sweet new friend at her favorite park. From experience, I know her fast-walk is energetically fueled by the depth of conversation and, of course, something hilarious too.

*unashamed* was written to bring a message about a Father's heart. This is a book to help all girls know what it really means to be a child of God. Getting to experience God as a father, is knowing a kindness that goes beyond anything this world has ever offered me. Knowing Him is knowing freedom, forgiveness, acceptance and daughtership. There is no room for SHAME in my relationship with Him. I am excited for girls just like me to read this book, and know they can be unashamed and confident in the One who says they are His own.

Caroline Levinson

# thanks

I am grateful to my daughter, Caroline and to Abby, Allie, Alyson, Amanda, Carlee, Callie, Baylor, Bree, Elissa, Emmie, Emily, my three Hannah's, Jessica, Kayla, Kaylee, Kelsie, Kimber, Lindsay, Lauren, Lydia, MacKenzie, Madelyn, Olivia, Sarah, Sterling, Sydney, and my treasured Tatum. To my son Joshua and to Andrew, Austin x 3, Blake, Conner, Chad, Chandler, Jared, John Allen, Josh, Mitchell, Ryan, and Sam x 2.

Deep gratitude goes to my grace teachers Leah Springer, John Sheasby, Andrew Farley, Paul White, Wayne Jacobson, the Apostle Paul and the mysterious writer of Hebrews. I was waiting for each and every one of you... Thank you for showing up in my life at just the right time and opening your mouth. Words can't suffice my gratitude for your teaching, I am forever changed.

A tapestry of friends walked closely beside me as I processed and produced this project. Thank you Tammy Anderson, Emily Alexander, Erica Andrews, Linda Carbonari, Kym Carter, Mary Forsythe, Colleen Foshee, Lisa Foster, Carolyn Franks, Karen Graham, Kim Hill, Lysle Holmes, Tammy Kling, Russell Lake, Aimee Larson, Sharon Lynch, Catherine Miller, Vicki Miller, Julie Musser, Kerrie and Phillip Oles, Steve and Wendy Riach, Ann Roberts, Victorya Rogers, Gina Roth,

Beverly Sheasby, Kristie Tillman, Amy Wahman, Margaret Weiss, and Kit Willock. If I have forgotten anyone, chalk it up to my dyslexia.

Tender gratitude goes to Anne Marie Coffee who selflessly offered her cool, and impressive graphic design talent to the cover of this project.

Special honor to Pastor Alan Smith, who suggested I write this book.

And to the love of my life, Mr. Bruce Levinson who spent countless hours listening to me and editing this book. You are my favorite. Thank you is not adequate. So, I will convince you of my gratitude later…

# unashamed

# about me

Hi. I'm Tracy.

I used to be an atheist. Here's my story. As a child, I was diagnosed with a severe learning disability. By the third grade, I was still not able to read. However, I had an inquisitive mind; constantly asking penetrating questions and analyzing all possible answers (I still do that…). This led me, at a young age, to question the existence of God. Years later, stimulated by a friend's threatened suicide, my path changed into being super curious about God. Now I'm a Jesus girl. The historical Jesus was so cool and wasn't anybody's "Yes" man. He challenged the religious systems of his day. He turned the world upside down and he sure did that for me.

The Bible is my favorite book. But, I believe it must be read carefully. Everything I believe is filtered through the message of the New Covenant, which I attempt to present in this book.

I also love speaking anywhere. That includes conferences, weekend retreats, podcasts, universities, basically anywhere the door opens for me to interact with people. Besides speaking and writing, I also get to know really cool people through interior design and teaching acting classes.

**unashamed**

Some people call all of this activity undiagnosed ADHD. I just call it, my life.

Finally, I'm crazy about my darling husband and my two children who have transitioned into my dearest pals. Check out our blog *outsidethenest* on tracylevinson.com.

**to connect with me**

I would love to hear from you. Maybe you would like me to speak at your event or maybe you just want to chat. My e-mail address is tracy@tracylevinson.com.

If you want to learn more about my thoughts about Jesus or my general frolicking, again go to my website, tracylevinson.com.

# unashamed book club/Bible study

I'm often "testing all things and holding fast to what is good". (1 Thessalonians 5:21). Perhaps it's because I come from a long line of attorneys. All supposed truths are on trial in my mind. I have this funny habit of thinking in Scripture. Often, when I make a statement, I like to back up the thought in my head with truth from the Bible, to the best of my understanding. It's super helpful in creating a Bible study. That is why you will see so many Scripture verses throughout this book. It is best to look at the context of each passage in the Bible mentioned by looking at surrounding verses. Also, remember what we studied about the New Covenant in the final chapter of this book. Often, to correctly divide the word of truth it is essential to consider what covenant the audience being addressed is under.

My hope is that groups of girls and women will gather and walk through this book together. It is set up in bite-sizes pieces that are manageable for small groups. As you hopefully share, laugh, and wrestle with these topics, you will have the opportunity to see exactly what Scripture I am considering as we journey together. Feel free to email me if you have any questions.

tracy@tracylevinson.com

**unashamed**

# notes

Chapter 1
F. Scott Fitzgerald, *This Side of Paradise* (New York: Scribner, 1920), 27-29.

Cathy Meyer, *Sexless Marriage: When Sex Ends at 'I Do,* Huffingtonpost.com, accessed Dec, 2015, www.huffingtonpost. com/cathy-meyer/sexless-marriage-when-sex_b_2280062.html.

Chapter 2
*The Oxford Pocket Dictionary of Current English.* (Oxford: Oxford University Press, 2009), accessed Dec. 2015, www.encyclopedia. com/doc/1O999-writhe.html.

Zig Ziglar quote, Ziglar.com, accessed December 2015, http://www. ziglar.com/quotes/chief-cause-failure-and-unhappiness.

Susan Donaldson James, "Baby Storm Raised Genderless Is Bad Experiment, Say Experts," abcnews.go.com, accessed December 16th, 2015, http://abcnews.go.com/Health/baby-storm-raised-genderless-gender-dangerous-experiment-child/story?id=13693760.

Frida Berrigan, "Who Needs Gender Norms? Not Children -- That's For Sure," Huffingtonpost.com, updated: October, 23, 2013, accessed December 16th, 2015, www.huffingtonpost. com/frida-berrigan/who-needs-gender-norms-no_b_3806302. html.

Chapter 3
Alan Smith, *Modesty and Beauty,* accessed December 2015, http://destinyinbloom.com/modesty-and-beauty/.

Pure Desire Ministries homepage, accessed December 2015, www.puredesire.org.

"Cambridge Study: Internet porn addiction mirrors drug addiction (2014)," yourbrainonporn.com, accessed December, 2015, http://yourbrainonporn.com/cambridge-university-brain-scans-find-porn-addiction.

Chapter 4

Ashley Strickland, *The lost art of offline dating*, updated February 12, 2013, accessed December 2015, www.cnn.com/2013/02/12/living/lost-art-offline-dating/

Anne Lamott. *Crooked Little Heart.* (New York: First Anchor Books, 1997), 185.

Victoria Rogers, *Finding a Man Worth Keeping* (),.

Chapter 6

Merriam Webster, Merriamwebster.com, accessed December 2015, www.merriam-webster.com/dictionary/obsolete.

N.T. Wright, *Surprised by Scripture,* (New York: HarperCollins. 2014), 226.

Andrew Farley, *The Naked Gospel* (Michigan: Zondervan, 2009), 56.

Frank Viola, *Jesus Now* (Colorado: David C. Cook, 2014), 41

John Sheasby, *The Birthright* ( Michigan: Zondervan, 2010), 131.

Andrew Farley, *The Naked Gospel* ( Michigan: Zondervan, 2009). 58.

Andrew Farley, *Relaxing with God* (Michigan: Baker Books, 2014), 38.

Josh Levinson, *Peace Like a River,* signed permission, 2015.

"Interview with Pastor, Professor and Author of *God without Religion*: Andrew Farley" Mattlitton.com, accessed December 2015, http://mattlitton.com/2011/06/24/.

John Sheasby, *The Birthright* (Michigan: Zondervan, 2010),  4.

Paul White, *Revelation to Transformation* (Indiana  WestBow Press. 2011),74-124.

"The Life of Howard G. "Prof' Hendricks," www.dts.edu, *DTS Magazine, Febuary 20, 2013, accessed December 2015,* www.dts.edu/read/howard-hendricks-prof.

Serendipity3, accessed on the homepage December, 2015, *www.serendipity3.com.*